Praise for *Turn This Car Around*

"Governor Ehrlich has delivered a concise, well-written road map on behalf of America's commonsense majority. This book is required reading for those who strive to restore the economy, culture, and reputation of America to its former greatness. And you won't find a finer foreword!"

—RUDY GIULIANI, "America's Mayor"
and former Mayor of New York City (1994–2001)

"Bob Ehrlich is one of the smartest Republican politicians in the country. And he has a lot to tell us in *Turn This Car Around*. It's both a compelling memoir of his time as Republican governor of a Democratic state and a riveting collection of political lessons he's learned. His advice on dealing with the media is especially persuasive."

—FRED BARNES, Executive Editor, *The Weekly Standard*

"Governor Ehrlich's frequent confrontations with special-interest groups in often hostile environments speak to his strength of character and strong leadership skills. This is a road map worth reading."

—GARY WILLIAMS, Coach of the University of Maryland
Men's Basketball Team, 2002 NCAA Tournament Champions

"*Turn This Car Around* offers a unique biographical and political perspective by a moderately conservative former governor of arguably the most liberal state in the union, Maryland. His accounts of riveting political battles, many of which he won despite the daunting political cards arrayed against him, is a tribute to Gov. Ehrlich's charisma, honesty, and political and rhetorical know-how."

—RICHARD E. VATZ, PH.D., Towson Distinguished Professor;
Associate Psychology Editor, *USA Today Magazine*;
Editor, *Current Psychology*

TURN
THIS CAR
AROUND

The Road Map
to Restoring America

TURN
THIS CAR
AROUND

GOVERNOR
Bob Ehrlich

BENBELLA

BENBELLA BOOKS, INC.

Dallas, Texas

BenBella Books, Inc.
10300 N. Central Expressway, Suite 400
Dallas, TX 75231
www.benbellabooks.com
Send feedback to feedback@benbellabooks.com

Printed in the United States of America
10 9 8 7 6 5 4 3 2 1

Library of Congress Cataloging-in-Publication Data

Ehrlich, Bob, 1957–
   Turn this car around : the road map to restoring America / by Governor Bob Ehrlich, former governor of Maryland.
       p. cm.
   Includes bibliographical references and index.
   ISBN 978-1-936661-55-8 (alk. paper)
   1. Ehrlich, Bob, 1957– 2. United States—Politics and government—1989– 3. United States—Social policy—21st century. I. Title.
   F186.35.E38A5 2011
   975.2'043092—dc23

                                                                    2011039173

Editing by Debbie Harmsen
Copyediting by Lisa Miller
Proofreading by Stacia Seaman and Michael Fedison
Cover design by Faceout Studio
Text design and composition by John Reinhardt Book Design
Printed by Berryville Graphics

Distributed by Perseus Distribution
(www.perseusdistribution.com)

To place orders through Perseus Distribution:
Tel: 800-343-4499
Fax: 800-351-5073
E-mail: orderentry@perseusbooks.com

Significant discounts for bulk sales are available.
Please contact Glenn Yeffeth at glenn@benbellabooks.com or (214) 750-3628.

To Kendel, my wife and best friend, who encouraged this project with her unfailing love from Day One; to Drew and Josh, who have brought such life and love to our family; and to Bob and Nancy Ehrlich, the parents who taught me what unconditional love is all about.

Contents

Acknowledgments

The wonderful obligation to acknowledge and thank those who contributed to this effort is mine and mine alone.

So, in no particular order, sincere thank-yous go out to:

Kendel Ehrlich
(supportive, beautiful, wonderful wife and mother)

Drew and Josh Ehrlich
(supportive, beautiful, and wonderful children)

Nancy and Bob Ehrlich Sr.
(the best parents in the world)

Henry Fawell
(loyal assistant, friend, and researcher)

Greg Massoni
(loyal agent, friend, and press flack)

Maura Teitelbaum
(agent and believer)

Chris Massoni
(*trusty assistant, scheduler, and proofreader*)

Paul Schurick
(*loyal aide, friend, and idea guy*)

Russ Schriefer
(*media consultant and friend*)

Elaine Pevenstein
(*trusty aide and godmother*)

Charles Krauthammer
(*friend and adviser*)

Fred Barnes
(*friend who encouraged this project*)

Professor Rick Vatz
(*friend who actually read the initial manuscript*)

Jared Monteiro
(*young aide, fact checker, and researcher*)

Patrick Mulford
(*young aide, fact checker, and researcher*)

Chrys Kefalas
(*former Ehrlich administration attorney*)

Glenn Yeffeth
(*publisher who believed in this book*)

Debbie Harmsen
(*helpful editor*)

Foreword

By the Honorable Rudy Giuliani

I MET THEN CONGRESSMAN BOB EHRLICH in 1996, around the time Bob was becoming an established star within the House GOP. Congressman Ehrlich's growing reputation as a thought leader and deputy whip made him a point person on behalf of various GOP priorities, from a federal balanced budget, to health care reform, to urban education.

His decision to leave a safe House seat in order to run against Kathleen Kennedy Townsend, the daughter of Bobby Kennedy, may not have been so popular in national GOP circles, but I stood and applauded Bob's willingness to compete against the daunting Kennedy machine in a dark blue state such as Maryland. My confidence paid off on November 5, 2002, as Bob Ehrlich became only the sixth Republican governor in Maryland history.

My appreciation for Bob's leadership abilities deepened during his tenure in Annapolis. Despite a hostile media and overwhelming Democratic control of the Maryland legislature, Bob became one of America's most successful governors.

Bob's independent streak ensured that his administration was not a garden-variety GOP operation, as his aggressive approach to criminal justice reform, drug policy reform, environmental stewardship, and people with disabilities etched out a unique and often unpredictable record for the Republican governor from Maryland.

His road map for a long-term, commonsense majority draws on Bob's experience in the private sector, state legislature, Congress, and governorship. His bitter battles with teachers' unions, environmental extremists, trial lawyers, and even members of his own party provide insight and perspective as to how a commonsense majority can assert its will in an increasingly politically correct culture.

This is Bob Ehrlich's first book and it defines a national cultural and economic agenda. It will not be his last...

INTRODUCTION

THE EXPERIENCE OF LOSING A RACE as an incumbent governor, with all of the accompanying indignities, has been one of the more difficult challenges life has thrown my way. However, out of every setback grows opportunity. In this case, I had more time to analyze the issues and prescribe solutions to the most controversial social, cultural, and economic issues of the day.

Two primary objectives were established at the beginning of the drafting process of this book. The first was to relate how one elected official's aggressive approach provides a timely example—a road map, if you will—to the preservation and possible expansion of a "conservative, common-values majority" in these politically correct times.

Indeed, the national debate surrounding the most critical issues in American politics has progressed in an even more divisive direction, as the Obama left and tea party–inspired GOP clash on a daily basis. And the stakes are quite high: the future of capitalism, a singular American culture, education policy for the new millennium, the health of race relations, the scourge of class envy, criminal justice reform, and the costs associated with a never-ending war on drugs is but a sampling of the controversies that must be addressed if we are to avoid the treacherous cliff that we are about to head off as a country—and culture.

The high-octane political conflicts described in these pages *can* empower a common-values majority to aggressively engage the modern left wherever and whenever their politically correct thought

1

police are deployed. That their efforts are focused on issues of class, race, ethnicity, and popular culture should come as no surprise; it is typically the most divisive social issues that excite them and their constituencies. I hope the retelling of these struggles from the perspective of one who held an elective office in a blue state adds a touch of realism, instruction, and entertainment value. Of these, instruction remains the most important. In this book I describe the elements of a midcourse correction intended to strengthen our culture, economy, and way of life. A more secure, commonsense-based governing majority will follow.

Commonsense values can win the public debate, particularly when the opposition has little to offer other than emotion and its progeny—class envy, political correctness, and a victim-based culture.

My other goal in writing this book was to produce a product that is truly mine—not the result of a Dictaphone and talented ghostwriter. It is said that the time-tested method of having someone else transcribe an author's words is the most widely used way to get oneself published; however, it was simply not the way I wanted to go about *my* business. This modus operandi is familiar; as governor of Maryland, I maintained the job of writing my major speeches. It was the way I felt most comfortable in delivering the spoken words. My initial attempt at crafting this first "masterpiece" would be no different.

The political showdowns that defined my time in public office were not always "fun." Constant media harping on my real or imagined failures to abide by a "PC" code of conduct was an annoyance. Opposition to populist causes that sound really good at first glance but have been proven to fail is heavy lifting for a Republican governor in a blue state. Persistent and sometimes ugly public fights might make for good press but tend to wear down even the most enthusiastic political warrior.

On the other hand, at no time did I buy into the view that I was elected to maintain the status quo. In fact, it was just the opposite. I understood my role to be one of compromise where needed, a quality my detractors would argue was in short supply, but confrontation where required—all in order to stay on offense. Commonsense values can win the public debate, particularly when the opposition has little to offer other than emotion and its progeny—class envy, political correctness, and a victim-based culture. Victory is never automatic; it takes a persistence and willingness to suffer serious indignities in order to prevail. In essence, this is the central theme of what is required on a national basis: constant engagement with the militant left will ultimately *Turn This Car Around*.

From the Sandlot to the State House

AN UGLY CONFRONTATION with the national Democratic Party was not exactly what I had in my mind when I spoke at the 2004 Republican National Convention in New York City. I was scheduled to deliver brief remarks to the Maryland delegation on the morning of August 29. I intended to be brief because I was scheduled to play golf at the world-famous Baltusrol Golf Club in nearby Springfield Township, New Jersey, later in the morning. My remarks were supposed to be a mere tune-up for then Lieutenant Governor Michael Steele's prime-time speech to the nation later that evening. Without the benefit of planning or calculation, however, I managed to turn what my staff thought would be a benign cheerleading session into a broadside at the national Democratic Party for its consistently successful use of race-baiting to divide the American electorate.

One remark stirred the pot more than any other: "I saw a message coming out of the Democratic convention: If you happen to have black skin, you have to believe one way. You have to. Or you are a traitor to your race.... That's racist."[1] My press staff immediately understood their time in New York City would be busier than planned; the initial phone calls from the national press corps began as I left the delegation meeting room. They did not stop for a week.

Democratic leaders in Maryland expressed sentiments reflective of the usual outrage, including this comment by Isiah Leggett, then chairman of the Maryland Democratic Party:

> What he has said and the way he has said it is tantamount to race-baiting.... He is saying that African-Americans, as opposed to other groups, are not intelligent enough and are so unsophisticated that they vote with the Democratic Party because they are too stupid to do otherwise.[2]

Of course, my remarks had no such purpose; they were directed at all Democratic operatives and pundits for their poor treatment of men such as Steele.

I, for one, had observed one too many instances of racial attacks targeted at any African American who dared to stray from the national Democratic Party. And this was my opportunity to give Democrats a taste of their own medicine—even if I did not fully appreciate the backlash my comments would generate at the time.

Indeed, such a direct shot at one of the most rock-solid Democratic establishments in America may not have been the most brilliant strategic move. I was only the sixth Republican governor in the 370-year history of a state that owned one of the most lopsided Democrat-to-Republican registration ratios in the country.

Nevertheless, Gregory Kane, the gifted and independent-minded African American columnist, saw my point and opined accordingly in *The Baltimore Sun*:

> Race-baiting is only to be practiced by Democrats. If Republicans want to engage in it, they have to fill out an official race-baiter

---

[1] David Nitkin, "Democrats 'Racist,' Md. Governor Says," *The Baltimore Sun*, August 31, 2004.
[2] Ibid.

application and get it witnessed and notarized by a bona fide Democratic Party apparatchik. A note from their mommies is also required.[3]

Fortunately, and to my great relief, my unscheduled sideshow did not overshadow Steele's extremely well-received speech. In fact, Steele's convention appearance marked a highlight in a four-year run that included major legislative successes on issues like school reform (our first legislative session brought the passage of a long-delayed charter school bill); Chesapeake Bay restoration; a balanced budget, including a multiyear budget surplus; and the establishment of a first-in-the-nation cabinet-level department devoted to the rights of people with disabilities. And all were accomplished working with a legislature where Republicans were outnumbered 141 to 47.

As usual, the "controversy" surrounding my observations died down rather quickly. This is no surprise since, as just about any casual observer remembers, Maryland Democratic leaders had regularly dismissed the first African American elected to statewide office. And therein lies a central tenet of this book and a core strategy for those on the front lines of our culture wars: direct confrontation wherever and whenever race-baiting tactics are used is the only way we will one day make racial politics less effective and a less permanent part of our political landscape. America will be better off for it, too.

A Blue-Collar Childhood

Some may view the emergence of a serious Republican from the "inner burbs" of Baltimore—Arbutus, Maryland—to be a unique case. My family's circumstances would tend to support this view. My father was a commission-only car salesman for thirty-seven years. My mother was a legal secretary until she retired at age sixty-seven. We had no family money to make a difference. It is a good bet there were no other Republicans living in the Kendale Apartments on Maiden Choice Lane other than Nancy Ehrlich. Mom's family had moved

---

[3] Gregory Kane, "When it comes to race baiting. Democrats are the guilty party," *The Baltimore Sun*, September 1, 2004.

from solidly Republican Lock Haven, Pennsylvania, to the solidly Democratic Baltimore suburb of Catonsville in 1947. And most certainly, there was no Republican blood on Dad's side of the family, where six kids were raised on a beat cop's salary smack dab in the middle of row house West Baltimore in the 1930s.

The lack of college degrees in our household did not dissuade plenty of political talk around the dining room table. Right-wing opinions from Dad, a former marine and Korean War combat veteran, dominated daily family conversations on the primary issues of the day, which ranged from Vietnam to civil rights and from crime to The Beatles. Despite Dad's Democratic registration (it took the McGovern campaign of 1972 to finally persuade Dad to switch parties), this conservative strain of thought was widely represented in working-class neighborhoods around the Baltimore Beltway. It was a Harry Truman/John Kennedy/Henry "Scoop" Jackson (later known as "Reagan Democrats") mentality. Voting patterns followed a Democratic path in local races and a decidedly Republican one in national elections. In an era before talk radio and 24/7 cable coverage, our constant family discussions made a strong imprint on an only child who early on became intrigued with the competitive nature of ideas, politics, and elections.

Like so many other kids similarly situated, I had no appreciation for the fact that our family had no money. My childhood was happy. Each day was filled with so many games of kickball, baseball, softball, tackle football, and basketball that I had neither the time nor the inclination to take a critical look around at my neighborhood.

If I had entertained such thoughts, I would have observed a small, thoroughly working-class apartment complex containing mostly white blue-collar families where the husband was employed by one of the area's large, industrial-era manufacturing plants that produced everything from beer and wine to aluminum siding. College educations were the exception; it was still the age when such an experience was viewed as more luxury than necessity.

Encouragement to speak one's mind during a tumultuous time in American history was also a neighborhood and family trait. The "Goldwater for President" bumper sticker on our apartment window, my mom walking me to the polls with a "Nixon's The One" banner draped around my shoulders, and watching and discussing the campus riots of '68 on our black-and-white television reflected intense parental interest and decidedly conservative opinions about world events.

It was also the constant drumbeat of a working-class work ethic, love of family, and sense of patriotism that crystallized the formative years for a boy growing up against the backdrop of the most turbulent decade of the American century.

The Influence of Sports

Like every other small community, Arbutus had plenty of sandlot ball—baseball in the spring, basketball in the winter, football in the fall—that generated a lot of excitement, community pride, and for me, opportunity. It was the type of opportunity Bob and Nancy Ehrlich could not have dared imagine while raising me in our small, one-hundred-dollar-a-month apartment. Who could have predicted that one day in 1971, Alan Abramson, my dad's boss, would talk about the ambition of a thirteen-year-old athlete from Arbutus Junior High School to Nick Schloeder, the head football coach at Gilman School, an exclusive private school then undertaking a serious outreach program to diversify its student body with "nontraditional students," i.e., blue-collar kids (mostly athletes) who were scholarship-eligible and could compete in the classroom?

The story relayed to Coach Schloeder was unique to the team I had made that year. The Arbutus 16–19 Big Red was made up of primarily eighteen- to nineteen-year-olds who had finished high school but wished to continue sandlot careers due to their love of the game or a desire to be scouted by a college coach in search of undiscovered talent. My situation was quite different in that my weight (185 pounds at age thirteen) made me ineligible for a more age-appropriate team. My options were clear: either play with a bunch of young men in a rough-and-tumble sandlot league or forgo football until I could enter high school in tenth grade at age fourteen. I chose to play.

Well, the unthinkable occurred in the space of a brief few weeks as Coach Schloeder attended one of my sandlot football games (one in which I got into a brief "altercation" with a member of the opposing team) and quickly extended an invitation to take Gilman's entrance exam, a difficult comprehensive test on which I performed well enough to qualify for admission. Soon thereafter, my life changed forever with an evening phone call from the director of admissions to my parents informing them that their son had been accepted to Gilman for the fall semester, and that scholarship money had been made available to meet most of the tuition costs.

Any thought of keeping with current plans vanished from my life at that very instant, as my still-stunned parents informed me that I would now be attending Gilman in the fall, not the local public high school I had planned to attend with my neighborhood friends.

And so began the critical turning point in my life, through which I would be exposed to powerful teacher-coach role models, a new set of friends, and a number of individuals who would open the door to limitless opportunities.

Entering High School

Gilman was a different place. It was located in an affluent part of northwest Baltimore, many miles from the familiar confines of small ranchers and row houses that dominated small-town Arbutus. Many of my classmates had been together since first grade. There were no girls. The dress code was coat and tie. There was daily homework. Academic standards were high, befitting an environment where every member of the senior class was expected to attend college—and quite selective colleges at that. The nightly crosstown commute was not fun, as I began arriving home hours after my neighborhood friends. Also, while there was no prohibition against my loud red-and-blue platform shoes—in vogue at that time in Arbutus—it was a style that I soon learned did not play well in my new school.

Despite this very different social environment and some initial struggles in the classroom, the Gilman experience left two essential lessons indelibly etched into my brain.

The first is that every individual, regardless of class, race, ethnicity, or religious conviction, has a right to be judged on his or her behavior and treatment of others—what Martin Luther King Jr. called "the content of their character." I was taught this lesson in part from athletics. Sports is a wonderful equalizer for young people in a new environment. The athletic field played a major part in creating a comfort zone while I acclimated to a strange and challenging new environment. Others in similar circumstances but lacking the leveling impact of athletics would have found this dramatic of a transition far more difficult. My teammates helped me gain acceptance and treated me as an equal, even though I came from more humble beginnings than many of the others on the field and court.

With one gigantic chip on my working-class shoulder, this first lesson from Gilman has proven invaluable given the variety of individuals encountered throughout my public life. My interaction with those of fundamentally different backgrounds taught me that I was no better, and no worse, than they were. As for that chip on my shoulder, it leveled over time, somewhere between a desperate need to prove myself in one of the most competitive schools in the state, and the constant reminder to take maximum advantage of the opportunities presented, a point driven home on a daily basis by Dad. "You *are* going to win," he would say. "You can't let down on that test. . . . You must compete hard to beat those guys." The lesson sank in. I was going to show everybody what I was made of every day. Failure was never an option.

Lesson two, which is the importance of mentors, is easily understood by anyone who has been impacted by powerful mentors at an impressionable age. My mentors in this case were teachers and coaches instrumental in securing my admission to Gilman, who, in turn, set high standards that I was expected to meet—no excuses.

Reddy Finney, a former football all-American center at Princeton, was the headmaster whose personality dominated every aspect of life at Gilman. "Mr. Finney" lived the ethics he always discussed during daily visits with his students. He knew every Gilman boy's name and his family circumstances. His presence generated rapt attention. He was "Mr. Chips comes to Baltimore"—a powerful and positive cult of personality extending into just about every facet of a Gilman student's life.

He followed my (and every Gilman boy's) progress closely and was always a cheerleader for my latest success on the field and in the classroom.

Other strong personalities were present as well. Coach Schloeder taught the most popular civics course at Gilman. Daily preparation was mandatory, particularly for "his" new kids on campus. His enthusiasm for public service and compassion for the poor became embedded in many generations of Gilman students. Alex Sotir, the new head football coach, drove his usually undersized prep school squad to repeated championships with equal parts sophistication and discipline. Sherm Bristow, the young basketball coach fresh out of Princeton (but raised in nearby blue-collar Parkville), was the cocky, wisecracking "buddy" one could engage in a daily test of athletic trivia. These and other teachers created a competitive yet balanced environment for young men fortunate enough to attend Gilman School.

These were intensely competitive individuals who wanted me to understand the doors that would be opened if my commitment was strong and consistent. In a real sense, their high expectations became *my* expectations. The thought of letting them down became unacceptable to me, whether in the classroom, on the playing field, or even at a Saturday night school dance. These expectations became a powerful motivation for the kid from the other side of the tracks. In retrospect, my buy-in was easy; they knew my circumstances and personality would not tolerate failure.

Heading to Princeton

These mentor-coaches helped me achieve a fair amount of high school athletic success, including selection to the all-metropolitan area baseball team and the all-state football team. Their insistence on academic performance was equally serious; my efforts earned admission to Princeton University, where a set of larger challenges awaited.

"Freshman Week" at Princeton brought a new roommate, community bathroom, placement tests, mass-produced meals, and a challenging academic schedule—as well as a week of football practice that brought more than fifty high school football captains and sixteen linebackers together to vie for two spots on the starting freshman defense. (This was prior to freshman eligibility in the Ivy League, which began in 1992.) The challenge drove my competitive nature, despite a size disadvantage that kept larger Division I schools from offering me "full ride" athletic scholarships. Again, a disciplined approach to the classroom and practice field led to two Princeton football captaincies (freshman and varsity), good grades, a senior thesis on everything you wanted to know about Alexander Solzhenitsyn (perhaps reflective of a nascent appreciation for an anti-authoritarian personality), and new respect for the opportunities presented by a world-class education and lifelong friendships.

Although a size deficiency would eliminate any serious thought of a career in the National Football League, one alternative plan at the time was to explore an extended college career in Canada with a hoped-for future shot at a Canadian Football League tryout. That dream ended in my senior year with a serious knee injury during a game against Colgate University.

It was a disappointing conclusion to a season that began with high hopes on a team and personal level. The resulting ACL surgery was a success, but I understood that competitive athletics would now be a part of my past. A new way to feed my competitive instincts had to be found. Little did I know that the next "game" would be played without a helmet, but I would feel plenty of contact just the same!

From the Football Field to a Courtroom

The recognition that a law degree would provide a good foundation in law, policy, and politics led me to Wake Forest Law School. I had the opportunity to fund my law school education through work as a part-time graduate assistant on the football staff. The part-time position was bottom-of-the-barrel stuff: supervising study hall, driving coaches to and from the airport, and breaking down game film. I loved it! I was able to finance my room and board and observe how two successful college football coaches, John Mackovic and Al Groh, ran a program that sought to compete in the Atlantic Coast Conference with high academic standards. Add in a tiny student body, and it is easy to understand why consistent football success at Wake is such a difficult task.

My job was time consuming, time that would have been better spent at the library for a first- and second-year law student. Time away from the books was not a major concern for me, however; even then my thought was to learn the law in order to better understand policy rather than secure a "billable hour" associate's position at a major law firm. The plan was to find a staff job on Capitol Hill.

Life took a different twist when a major Baltimore law firm—Ober, Kaler, Grimes & Shriver—offered an associate's position after a brief clerkship over Christmas vacation in 1982. The starting salary of $30,500 sounded like all the money in the world to me—and it was. My graduate assistant's salary at Wake Forest had been $240 a month (plus all the food I could eat at the team's training table).

The opportunity to work for a well-regarded firm and gentlemen attorneys in my hometown was another piece of good luck. Volunteer efforts in several local GOP campaigns and the long work hours of a large firm associate meant I was rarely home but always busy. Despite the trials and tribulations of this learning experience and the concerns of some partners about my career path ("Does he really want to be an attorney?"), I was treated well at Ober, made lifelong friends, and learned to write at a higher level—a skill often lacking in college graduates today.

My rather rare courtroom appearances as a litigation associate were not enough to feed my competitive drive. So, after three years of a typical associate's life—long hours, billable requirements, and concerns about a partnership track—I set my sights on what had been on my mind since college: a run for the Maryland state legislature.

The Political Bug Bites

Most political observers thought the task impossible, and they had a good point. How else do you view a twenty-eight-year-old novice with no money running in a primary against an entrenched three-term, three-member incumbent team (most Maryland House districts are represented by multiple delegates) in a solidly Republican district? Not to mention the fact that I was a recent arrival, having lived in a neighboring district for only the past three years.

My new district encompassed the northern suburbs of Baltimore County all the way to the Pennsylvania line. Although Republican members were an insignificant minority in the Maryland General

Assembly, what passed for a Republican political base was this tenth legislative district with its middle-class town house developments and large horse farms. The race would focus on the primary election, as Democrats were viewed as noncompetitive in the general one. Still, everyone in my camp understood it would take a serious, disciplined effort to win.

Despite the odds, and against the wishes of some local Republican leaders I launched an aggressive and sophisticated (at the time, at least) eighteen-month campaign—and won! My first election night was nerve-racking, as the returns reflected a close race for the third and final spot on the ticket. The final margin was a miniscule ninety votes. The well-executed, grassroots-focused, targeted effort confounded the pundits, angered some elements of the local press, and turned on many heretofore uninterested voters. The message was "new leadership" (in reality a newly aggressive leadership), and a decidedly libertarian bent to familiar GOP themes of fiscal restraint, legal reform, and criminal sanctions. I enjoyed the "outsider" label, one which harkened back to my days of walking the halls of Gilman and Princeton. I again came to appreciate what a handful of properly motivated and well-led people with a bit of an attitude (that old chip on the shoulder hadn't completely disappeared) could accomplish when presented with an opportunity—even a long-shot opportunity.

An eight-year, thoroughly educational experience followed, in which I learned my new craft while working both sides of the partisan divide in a citizen legislature then known for its collegial style. In the process, I was quickly educated to the growing division between the traditional, blue-collar, socially conservative Democratic Party members I became natural allies with and the newly emerging, hard-left party controlled by public labor unions, the trial bar, feminist groups, and anti-growth environmentalists. For context, begin with Harry Truman and end with Howard Dean. Fortunately, this was still a time when a majority of right-leaning Democrats formed coalitions with generally conservative Republicans to get things done or, at times, defeat the worst inclinations of the left.

I thrived in this environment, although my initial committee assignment was not to my liking. Against my wishes, I was assigned to the House Judiciary Committee, a rather infamous panel known for its willingness to kill even popular pieces of legislation, but which included some of the brightest and most able attorneys in the General Assembly. It was during this time that I was adopted by senior Democratic leaders who took an interest in my career. As a result, my bills were passed, and I was made a part of the "backroom group" charged with deciding which amended bills the committee would send to the floor of the House. This was still a time when even substantive bill language was drafted by the member, rather than committee staff, a practice now so dominant in many state legislatures and especially in U.S. House committees.

I recall this time in the Maryland House Judiciary Committee as the most enjoyable of my twenty years in public life. The committee leaders then included strong conservatives such as Chairmen Bill Horne, Danny Long, and John Arnick. I received a daily lesson in many areas of the law that were outside my practice area and came to appreciate how difficult it was for so many of my colleagues to balance their country law office practices with the demands of public office. The special benefits of a part-time citizen legislature became apparent as well, as the trend toward more full-time assemblies and a more aggressive spending mindset began to take root in legislatures around the country. Unfortunately, full-time state legislators tend to become more removed from real-world experiences; it's always healthier to have members who live, work, start businesses, and pay taxes in the real world. Our forefathers certainly foresaw what damage a full-time legislature might inflict!

Congressional Hot Seat

On the career front, what followed was completely unexpected, although some had predicted it as far back as high school.

"It" was a run for the U.S. Congress to represent Baltimore's northern and eastern suburbs in Maryland's Second Congressional District. The seat was being vacated by the popular Republican Helen Delich Bentley, the crusty former newspaper reporter who had established a name for herself while covering the Baltimore waterfront in the 1950s and 1960s. Her love for the Port of Baltimore, reputation for hard work, and appeal to crossover, working-class Democrats had

Bob Sr. and Bob Jr. in D.C. at swearing-in day for the 104th Congress.

catapulted her into Congress in 1984 after two close but unsuccessful attempts.

In 1986, she easily beat back a challenge from Kathleen Kennedy Townsend, Robert F. Kennedy's daughter and a relative newcomer to Maryland in search of her first elected public office. For me, Bentley's decision to run for governor in 1994 meant a matchup against a neighboring Baltimore County delegate, Gerry Brewster. Brewster's father, Daniel B. Brewster, had been a war hero and popular U.S.

senator until his support for an increasingly unpopular war and his drinking problems led to his defeat in 1968.

The younger Brewster was rightly seen as a rising star in the Maryland Democratic Party and a tough opponent for his father's old second district seat in Congress. The drama was heightened by the particulars of the matchup: two thirtysomething attorneys, classmates in high school, classmates in college, and committee-mates in the Maryland General Assembly's House of Delegates were now head-to-head in one of the few competitive congressional districts left in Maryland. The press ate it up, and both national party committees poured money into what most political observers believed would be a close race.

In early summer 1994, when our first poll showed Brewster up by fifteen points, some members of our campaign staff feared I would be disappointed, given the difficulty of the race and the assumed fund-raising advantage of the Brewster family political machine. This was not the case. I suspected we could win, and win comfortably, in light of a newly redrawn district that had a solid Republican base and an abundance of Reagan Democrat, blue-collar neighborhoods, a relentless appearance schedule, and a well-executed campaign that would relate my life story in startling contrast to Brewster's more privileged résumé. My personal relationships across the aisle paid dividends as well. Many Democratic officeholders in and around Baltimore either sat on their hands or openly supported our campaign. Those long hours sitting in the House Judiciary Committee and a willingness to work with right-leaning Democrats in the General Assembly were now paying off.

One additional obstacle in our way was the issue of family entitlement, the notion that this was a family seat "reserved" for the next generation of the Brewster family. In a machine state such as Maryland, I knew this idea had to be taken down before it could gain momentum. Accordingly, it was challenged at every opportunity as I aggressively attacked the idea that there could be an entitlement to anything as important as a seat in Congress. The stakes were even higher because of the large shoes I was now expected to fill as Helen Bentley's successor. Her brand of Republican populism had proven to be extremely popular in the conservative Democrat neighborhoods of Eastern Baltimore County. She had saved the Maryland Republican Party in the leanest of times. I was now expected to grow the party during the best of times.

Here again, the atypical, blue-collar Republican campaign with a strong comfort level in union, Democratic precincts resulted in a resounding victory—a startling 63 percent to 37 percent win. The failure of "Hillarycare" and Bill Clinton's lagging poll numbers did not hurt, either, as Republicans reclaimed the House of Representatives for the first time in forty years. Election night was magical, as I would be the sole freshman Republican from Maryland to take a seat in the historic 104th Congress.

One memory stands out among all others from that exciting night. As we pulled up to the Administration Building on the grounds of the Maryland State Fairgrounds, I turned to my wife, Kendel, and asked if she was ready for what we knew would be a *really big change* in our life. Of course, the answer was "yes." Kendel Ehrlich is always on board and ready to go—not a surprising view given that our initial meeting took place on Election Day 1990 at a polling place near her home in Riderwood, Maryland. Only later would I learn that my wife-to-be had in fact supported me in my attempt to be reelected to the Maryland legislature that day. You see, our initial introduction (by a mutual friend) had occurred *after* she had voted and was hurrying to her car!

A New Chapter in D.C.

After the obligatory new member retreat held in Baltimore and sponsored by the Heritage Foundation, rather than at Harvard and sponsored by the Kennedy School of Government, as was past practice, it was off to Capitol Hill and a promising new era in American politics.

On a personal level, there were many life-impacting decisions that had to be made in a brief period of time: the hiring of congressional staff, the redesign of an ongoing campaign operation, the shutting down of a law practice, the location of an apartment on Capitol Hill, and a decision on a new career path for my public defender wife. These issues and many more had to be addressed during the two-month run-up to the start of the 104th Congress in January 1995.

In retrospect, the decisions we made during that wild time were pretty good ones, with the notable exception of Kendel leaving her district public defender's position without first securing a new job. We soon learned that much of the interest in her was more a function of my new position and not her considerable legal talents. Fortunately, she (we) soon discerned the landscape and rejected the idea of a D.C. law firm position; the conflict-of-interest issues presented by a member's spouse working for well-known lobbyists were too plentiful—and obvious. Why generate a public relations nightmare right out of the box? In the end, she accepted an assistant prosecutor position in Harford County, Maryland, where she found unexpected happiness on the other side of the table in a friendly and supportive courthouse.

I quickly came to realize this was a place marked by partisan lines in every respect, with the exception of the House gym, where well-earned sweat seemed to breach the partisan divide during daily pickup basketball games.

A new majority, Newt Gingrich, the Contract with America, an emerging friendship with fellow freshman Congressman Sonny Bono, membership on the House Banking and Financial Services Committee, and constant media attention marked the beginning of an eventful and successful four terms in the House. Quite unlike the Maryland legislature, I quickly came to realize this was a place marked by partisan lines in every respect, with the exception of the House gym, where well-earned sweat seemed to breach the partisan divide during daily pickup basketball games.

The party-line votes that were novel to me but so expected in this political culture followed the outbreak of more ideological political party control in the modern era, with 90 percent of Republican members qualifying as conservative and 90 percent of Democrats leaning liberal. The resulting political environment was one of resentment, hardball tactics, and intense philosophical debate—often crossing the line into the personal.

One of the worst aspects of this culture was the abuse of the ethics process to impeach character and ruin reputation, a practice turned into an art form by both parties. This was the single most negative aspect of my new work environment, and one that will always taint my view of Congress. No political victory could be worth the destructive behavior a few of my colleagues showed toward others within a system allegedly immune from misuse. For a few, partisan participation in the ethics process became blood sport, with the singular goal of personally damaging one or more individuals from the other party. In retrospect, the state of things should not have been a surprise in a place where majority/minority status has an impact on just about every aspect of daily life. Moreover, it was payback time for long-suffering congressional Republicans consistently abused by the Democratic leadership over the past forty years. Control of the Rules Committee would ensure party-line procedural votes, and the leadership would continue to limit knowledge of proposed House action to GOP members. Only a personal friendship would guarantee advance notice of the next week's floor schedule for a Democratic member.

The evolution of clearly identifiable philosophical control within the respective parties made real debate and, in most cases, real compromise nearly impossible. For example, the demise of so many "Blue Dog" Democrats since the Reagan years made consensus and bipartisan coalitions increasingly unlikely on issues such as Medicaid reform, elimination of the federal estate tax, a capital gains tax cut, and criminal justice reform.

The increasing politicization of the ethics process and a stark ideological divide serve to discourage many qualified candidates from entering politics. So many political aspirants ask, "Who needs this stuff? Why risk my good name in a business where character assassination is such an accepted part of the job description?"

For me, a high-stakes competition requires some level of fair play or, at the very least, the belief that lines must be drawn when individual integrity is at stake. Integrity here is much more than the classic definition of doing the right thing when nobody is looking; it means not crossing the line into frivolous attacks when everybody is looking.

Despite this poisonous political culture, my eight years in the House were interesting and productive. The experience provided firsthand insight and involvement in signature events in American history, including passage of federal welfare reform, a balanced budget, the siege at Waco, impeachment, 9/11, and Iraq. As a member who continued to draft major policy position papers in my own hand, the intellectual aspect of the congressional experience made every day as interesting as the day before. It was a daily dose of substance, much like a series of college seminars, and I did not even have to pay tuition. Nevertheless, my vote was but one of 435—not the type of impact I desired to have on a daily basis. My longer-term concerns about impact were further exacerbated by the suspicion that my more libertarian views on many social issues (a policy "exam" on the threshold issues of abortion and guns followed by both parties) would keep me out of a leadership position, perhaps forever.

On the flip side, there was a lot to appreciate about my place in the world. Our first son, Drew, had been born in July 1999. By then I was enjoying life in a "safe seat" close to Capitol Hill with an assignment to a prestigious "A" committee, the House Energy and Commerce Committee. Fund-raising would not be a concern, and my committee assignment meant a constant dose of major policy issues would come my way. Further, I had access to the leadership through my position in the whip organization (a group tasked with counting votes on legislation), a position I could use to secure favors for my district. So now that I was ensconced in a terrific district with a supposedly bright future, all was well with the world, right? Well, not exactly.

Politics amid the War on Terror

In the fall of 2001, post-9/11, the decades-long terror war against the West was just beginning to be understood by the American public. The need for leadership was in high demand, the state of Maryland was mired in a budget mess of historic proportions, a gubernatorial election was looming just over the horizon, and many Maryland GOP activists were demanding to know my future plans. "Plans" in this context meant a final decision on whether I would make the jump into the race for governor in 2002. The situation called for real soul-searching, including the need to address a series of questions I might have decided to bypass under normal circumstances.

As the pressure mounted. a few of the obvious issues appeared on a daily basis: What about the comfort level of my safe seat? Would I miss the daily action and regular victories over the Democrats? Would I enjoy an executive position? Did I have the attitude and talent to be an executive? How could I escape from the "little stuff" in order to spend time on the "big stuff"? Could I convert a reliably hostile print media to at least neutral? Could a Republican win state-wide in Maryland? Could I raise enough money to compete against the Kennedy money machine, which was in full motion in support-ing presumptive Democratic nominee Kathleen Kennedy Townsend? These were just a few of the difficult questions crisscrossing my mind during the summer and fall of 2001.

All of the influences that had played a part in my life came to-gether during that time of decision. This was the ultimate competi-tion for a Maryland Republican—the opportunity to compete against a Kennedy in a dark blue state; the notion that a working-class Republican with an appeal to suburban, middle-class voters might have a chance, *if* the execution were near perfect, *if* the political envi-ronment were good enough, and *if* our proposed message—*"It's time for a change"*—could resonate.

The "ifs" were daunting, but the foundation was rock solid. My wife, Kendel, was the strongest advocate for the move, a major con-sideration given the strength of our marriage and the central role she would need to play in appealing to women voters, a reliably Democratic voting bloc harboring increasingly strong suspicions about organized religion's role within the national and state GOP. Party leaders across the state and country signaled their support, an easy position to assume since *they* were not giving up a safe seat in Congress to chase a highly unlikely victory.

A few months of severe tension headaches (with nightly grind-ing of teeth thrown in for good measure) was the painful backdrop for my decision-making process. The strong push from support-ers to "go for it" was negated by the pull from House leadership to keep a safe seat in a tough state in Republican hands. Close friends such as then House Speaker Dennis Hastert and then National Republican Campaign Committee Chairman Tom Davis made seri-ous pleas to forgo what they expected to be a nearly impossible run. I understood their position on a personal and political level, as the near-forty-year gubernatorial losing streak in Maryland appeared to be an insurmountable obstacle.

Over time, however, a central fact of political life became quite clear: this was probably the best statewide opportunity I would ever be presented with, despite the long odds against success. If not now, most likely never. If not now, I could stop fooling myself into believing a high-stakes statewide campaign was in my future. "Never" is an awful long time. My answer had to be "yes." This had to be the time to risk "safe" for a larger challenge.

On March 25, 2002, surrounded by hundreds of former neighbors, classmates, teammates, friends, and supporters, I stood on my parents' tiny front lawn in Arbutus to announce my candidacy for governor of Maryland. As the cameras rolled and Drew tried to figure out what was going on around Mom-Mom's lawn, I spoke of the need for change in a one-party state whose leadership was engaged in the worst kind of "spend and tax" politics: where the spending comes first and the tax increases come later, after the election. I was nervous but confident about what could be accomplished. We were ready to take control. We were ready to lead. But was Maryland ready for a radical change? Where were we going to find the votes to win, and what about all that money we would need to carry us to victory?

Our initial polling was not promising, as reflected when Glen Bolger of Public Opinion Strategies, our pollster since 1993 and a veteran of Maryland politics, convened a meeting of our finance committee in which he presented his baseline poll in the late fall of 2001. The results? Fifty-one percent of those polled would vote for Townsend and only 29 percent would vote for me. Glen's message that night made a lasting impression: this was an almost impossible race in light of the two-to-one Democrat-to-Republican party ratio, large Democratic majorities in the General Assembly, a popular female incumbent lieutenant governor, and increasingly Democratic trend lines in the populous suburbs of Washington, D.C. He added that we had an "outside" chance to win, "with 51 percent," *if* everything went right for us and wrong for them, but even then we would have to "get lucky." Wow, and this was *our* guy?

The dour nature of the meeting served its intended purpose. I needed everyone in attendance to understand the challenge present-ed by the race. "All hands on deck" was to be a minimum require-ment if we were to pull off the upset.

The decision was made, the necessary papers were filed, and life changed again, forever.

If contrast is your thing, then *this* was your kind of race: man ver-sus woman; Republican versus Democrat; conservative versus lib-eral; Arbutus, Maryland, versus Hyannisport, Massachusetts; family row house versus family compound; outsider versus establishment; change versus status quo; and perhaps most important, risk versus entitlement. The prevailing view across Maryland, even among some of my supporters, was that Kathleen Kennedy Townsend was next in the Kennedy family line—even *entitled*—to be governor of this dark blue state. And the blue-collar Republican congressman from Maryland's tiny minority party was *risking it all* to reach a seemingly impossible goal.

The contrast worked at every stage, often to a startling degree. This was perhaps nowhere more clear than when a ticket to a $2,000 per-person clam bake fund-raiser at the Kennedy family compound found its way to the Ehrlich campaign headquarters. What better contrast to this high-dollar, out-of-state event than a $25 per-person crab feast to be held at the well-worn Arbutus Town Hall, complete with lobster T-shirts emblazoned with the universal sign of disapproval through its crab claws? This was a no-brainer, and we played the contrast-ing events to the hilt. At our event, the crabs were plentiful, as were the patrons. Everyone was in a good mood. Local television stations dispatched correspondents to Hyannisport and Arbutus. One corre-spondent reported from outside the cold and unfamiliar walls of the Kennedy compound, while another reported from inside the warm, loud, and no-frills Arbutus Town Hall.

Subtle? Not at all. Effective? Absolutely. The Kennedy campaign cried foul, our campaign had a good laugh, and our message that "it's time for a change" began to take hold. We hammered relentlessly on the need for change from a sloppy, arrogant monopoly to a com-petitive two-party state. We promised to produce a thriving market-place of ideas; change that would reject the Democrats' increasingly hard-left orientation so out of touch with those hardworking blue-collar suburbs around Baltimore—like Arbutus.

Winning and What We Learned

A series of fascinating events took place in that summer and fall of 2002, a number of which will be explored in future chapters. They contain lessons to be learned if a still too silent majority of Republican, Democratic, and Independent conservative-leaning Americans is to challenge and defeat an increasingly liberal, politically correct establishment bent on remaking American culture. This radical remaking of American culture *can* be defeated with a massive dose of common sense and the courage to accept short-term consequences when the PC police and their supporters in the media and academia conduct attack operations. The tone of these operations is unusually unpleasant because a permanent lesson is meant to be taught by the so easily offended left. The ability to survive such attacks in the short term, while redefining terms along the way, is the key to long-term success. This was my formula from 1987 to 2006. I submit it as a recipe for the preservation and renewal of our popular culture going forward.

My instincts that we could win came to pass on November 5, 2002, as Maryland elected a Republican governor for the first time in thirty-six years. The victory margin of approximately seventy thousand votes was not exactly a landslide, nor was it the razor-thin outcome that Glen Bolger saw as the most optimistic scenario at the outset of the race. It was a clear example of what the Republican base and disenfranchised moderate Democrats could achieve in a conducive environment.

Thus began an opportunity to effect change within a political culture for the first time in a very long time. The impact was significant, as we seized the opportunity not only to challenge a long-standing political monopoly but also take down a number of the left's sacred cows in the process. The story and lessons of this historic challenge, with its successes and failures, are the reasons I wrote this book. I hope you enjoy it.

Taking On
the Language Battle

IN THE SPRING OF 2003 I stood before a class of eighty Towson University students in the popular Persuasion class taught by rhetoric and communication professor Richard Vatz. I had been a guest lecturer in the class twice a year since I was first elected to Congress in 1994. Press coverage of my visits was guaranteed, as reporters knew I would provide blunt responses to difficult but fair questions from students. I enjoyed these sometimes-controversial visits because the Towson students were usually responsive to my requests for aggressive debate on the issues of the day. I would argue about any issue or policy, as long as supporting facts were offered. The difference between fact and opinion was debated at great length, too. My point was always to encourage independence when taking a position; opinions and influence from Mom, Dad, Professor Vatz, or Fox News did not count.

But today was different. It was my first lecture since being elected governor. I wanted to put the students to a different test.

"Raise your hand if you are pro-life," I said. Slowly, a couple dozen hands went up, some with confidence, some with reticence.

"Okay, hands down. Now raise your hand if you are pro-choice." Again, hands slowly went up. A few students checked to see where on the controversial fence their friends and classmates had landed.

"Congratulations. You're all wrong," I said. "Here's why. Every one of you who raised your hand allowed me, a guy you've never met and only seen on TV, to define your beliefs. You walked right into a debate on the sensitive topic of abortion without requesting that I define the terms 'pro-life' and 'pro-choice.' In effect, you allowed the questioner [me] to control the discussion because only I knew what I meant by those hot-button phrases.

"What about late-term abortions? Under which exceptions would you approve Medicaid [public] funding of abortions? What about parental notification versus parental consent? Did you think about judicial bypass? Had you considered exceptions in cases of rape, incest, or where the life of the mother is at stake? What about the abortion debate's relation to stem cell research? If you raised your hand, you truly had no defined concept of what I was talking about. And in competitive politics, you would pay a steep price for taking a stand on a controversial topic with varying interpretations, regardless of which side of the issue you support."

The lesson: always fight the inclinations of your opponents to define you, your votes, and your convictions. The battlefield of campaigns and elections is littered with the bodies of candidates who let their opponents define their positions and their records.

For instance, in my 2002 campaign for governor I successfully defined the fiscal consequences of thirty-six years of one-party rule. I argued that the budget crisis crippling state government was the result of a sloppy, arrogant monopoly in power for far too long. Conversely, Democrats in the 2006 election cycle successfully branded Republican candidates across the country as "corrupt," whether they had met Jack Abramoff or not, and they (and yours truly) paid the price at the ballot box. Like these unfortunate Republicans, the students at Towson University learned the value of language the hard way, but before it really counts—in real life.

I informed the students that their opponents will often sink to disgraceful depths as a means of defining them. No example is more pertinent than *The Baltimore Sun* editorial board opining in 2002 that my African American running mate and future lieutenant governor, Michael Steele, added "little to the ticket but the color of his skin."[4] Rather than engage Steele and me on the issues, the editorial pegged him as a "token" not worthy of statewide office. This could have been an effective strategy if one, we had not made an immediate, aggressive response; and two, we had not repeatedly characterized this incident as defining what the *Sun's* editorial board was truly all about, particularly its intolerance toward an "inconvenient" individual such as Steele. In the absence of our aggressive reaction, we would have been forced on the defensive and required to debate Steele's image problem prior to engaging in a real debate on the issues of the day.

"Don't you ever let anyone do to you what *The Sun* tried to do to Michael Steele, ever," I told the students.

One last point about that visit to Towson. Before Professor Vatz dismissed the students that day, I asked for another quick show of hands: "Who's pro-gun?" No one raised a hand. Now *that's* persuasion.

The Business of Words

Our choice of words is important when we debate the issues of the day. Historically, this has been a problem for the right because its principles often constitute a more challenging sell, made all the more difficult as a relentless left seeks to capture the moral and emotional high ground on every issue.

An excellent example can be observed in the words and rhetoric surrounding the debate on raising the minimum wage. Similar observations can be made about so-called "living wage" legislation. (More on the "demerits" of this initiative in Chapter 17.) In both cases, the language typically used to describe the issues compels the

---

[4] Editorial, "Townsend for Governor," *The Baltimore Sun*, November 3, 2002.

reader or observer to a particular conclusion: Could *you* live on six dollars per hour? How could you feed *your* kids? It's not fair that CEOs make millions while others make minimum wage! Where is your sense of compassion? How could *you* so easily forget where you came from? You are just a mean-spirited Republican!

Job losses are usually sustained by marginal workers when the cost of labor rises. But an otherwise rational economic argument about the increase in unemployment that comes from raising the minimum wage has no chance against the emotionally charged words used by proponents of a wage hike. It frequently does not even get raised. Similarly, when Republicans in the 104th Congress advocated slowing the growth in certain entitlement programs, particularly Medicare, the left successfully characterized the proposals as "cuts." Smaller increases to what had been promised in certain entitlement programs are not cuts; neither are they easy to explain once the thirty-second attack ads begin.

Think about how the right and left go about their daily fight for public approval: Conservatives typically say *no*; liberals say *yes*. Conservatives say *less*, liberals say *more*. Conservatives say *tolerate*, liberals say *accept*. The right advocates the intangibles—*freedom, autonomy, responsibility,* and *opportunity*—while liberals market the tangibles—*programs, departments, bureaus, agencies,* and *lawsuits*—to "solve" societal problems.

Defining Ourselves

After countless debates on the more sensitive issues of the day, I hereby submit a series of definitions, and more importantly, distinctions, on the core issues of the day that libertarians and anyone on the right should think about in making and taking our case to the public.

(1) **We support affirmative action (when warranted), not quotas.** I am an affirmative action kid, given the substantial financial aid dollars provided to me and my parents throughout high school, college, and law school. Economic assistance that opens doors otherwise closed to a member of a certain socioeconomic class or race is a classic form of affirmative action, and one that is easily understood and accepted by the vast majority of Americans. Compare this notion to

one that seeks to provide special, guaranteed results on the basis of sex, ethnicity, or race. This is a much less acceptable concept—and one guaranteed to generate resentment. Moreover, it is always useful to remind one's audience what the courts have said regarding guaranteed results and "set aside" programs: such initiatives are lawful only where demonstrable vestiges of discrimination exist. No more, no less.

(2) **We support inclusion, not preference.** Here again, a major distinction exists. Inclusion denotes removal of barriers to ensure access; preference presupposes a desire for a particular result. Preference is simply a lesser form of quota, and the foregoing analysis applies equally here.

(3) **We advocate for conservation, not environmental extremism.** There is a world of difference between conservation-minded "Ducks Unlimited" and the left-leaning "Sierra Club." One advocates for preservation and conservation. The other is a mainstay of the "no growth" mindset. The former is never cited as an environmental advocacy group; the latter is a favorite for those of a more "progressive" mindset. Note how any preservation or conservation group associated with Second Amendment rights is never described as "environmentally friendly."

(4) **We are multiethnic but not multicultural.** This *should* be a no-brainer. Unfortunately, in contemporary America, it is not. We are a nation of immigrants, respecting many different ethnic backgrounds brought together, sometimes by force, in order to assimilate into a common culture. Such is our melting pot culture, a culture singularly identifiable as the "American culture." For a more complete analysis of this problem, see Chapter 4, "Taking On the Multicultural Police."

(5) **We reject any and all attempts to narrow the definition of "conservative."** Many left-leaning journalists and pundits fall easily into the role of "definition police" through their compulsion to summarily and narrowly define someone on the right in order to quickly dismiss them. The reason they do this goes far beyond a simple desire to win a philosophical argument or browbeat a political opponent. Many years of observation have led me to a disquieting but impossible-to-miss conclusion: this dismissive attitude is a

defensive mechanism to ensure against any attempt at counterintuitive analysis. In my public life, this attitude has manifested itself in an inability to digest the substance of positions taken outside of what a "conservative," "Republican," or "libertarian" legislator, congressman, or governor is "supposed" to believe or represent.

Consider the following analysis piece that appeared in *The Baltimore Sun* a little more than a month after I was sworn in as Maryland's sixtieth governor. The headline read "Weighing Ehrlich's move to the middle." The story proceeded to analyze how my "moderate" positions on social issues were in reality Democratic positions I was seeking to co-opt because of the realities of blue-state Maryland. Senate President Mike Miller was cited as a frustrated Democratic leader who was having a difficult time differentiating his party's program from mine because of the "Democratic themes" I had sounded out in my first State-of-the-State address in 2003.

The most striking aspect of the story was the list of issues cited in support of my alleged turn to the middle. The agenda items included increased aid for the mentally ill, (employment) support for people with disabilities, programs to keep nonviolent substance abuse offenders out of prison, tax credits for historic preservation, and support for the decriminalization of medical marijuana. While most of these issue positions are examined in greater detail later in this book, it would have taken little effort to learn that these were long-standing positions of mine dating back to my service in the Maryland General Assembly and the U.S. Congress. Moreover, I have found few self-identified conservatives who oppose government intervention on behalf of those who are unable to take care of themselves. Yet the story focused on the political motivation behind my moves to placate moderate Marylanders. From my perspective, the real story would have been if I had repudiated these long-standing positions in order to secure political goodwill on the right!

This analysis piece reminded me of how the interpretative process worked with so many of the reporters who covered me on a daily basis. Because so many of my views on social issues were examples of where my actual position did not reflect the assumed Republican position, a dissidence/denial response was generated. This response

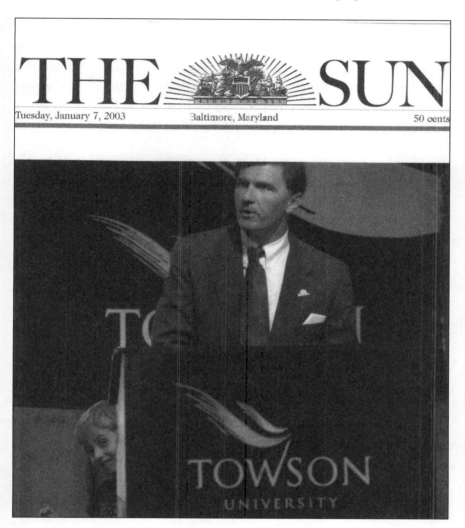

THE ☀ SUN

Tuesday, January 7, 2003   Baltimore, Maryland   50 cents

Drew Ehrlich, at age 3, takes a peek from behind the lectern during his father's presentation of congressional papers to Towson University.

was always interesting to observe as reporters chose to disregard or explain away ("he has to run to the middle") opinions and positions outside of their partisan prisms. The denial is in direct response to the dissidence because it is the initial and easiest reaction for those who do not wish to think or operate outside their ideological straightjackets.

Racial stereotyping is the most common context in which this refusal to recognize facts outside of one's political lens is observed. Such examples are plentiful in race-centric states like Maryland. A number of these instances are explored in greater detail in Chapter 7, "Taking On the Race Card."

Periodic clashes with the definition police serve as one of the consistent story lines in this book. The obvious downside was to suffer very public slings and arrows from those afflicted with the syndrome, particularly journalists employed by *The Baltimore Sun* and *The Washington Post*. The stimulating upside was to expose, engage, and attempt to rebuff those who sought to damage me or those associated with me through their unbending partisan focus. Sometimes we won and sometimes we lost. We seldom failed to engage, however.

(6) **We are compassionate but do not celebrate dysfunction.** When did compassion get confused with the notion of nonjudgmental dysfunction? When did our values become so twisted that a conditionless societal contract is seen as the cultural norm? Homelessness, teen pregnancy, social promotion, and political correctness are the problems, the by-products of an increasingly valueless society. In other words, our natural compassion must not be overridden by the increasingly accepted idea of a standardless society. Volumes have been written about misplaced compassion generating dependence on government programs and taxpayer dollars. Cottage industries have grown up around the culture of victimization. The fuel driving our culture's relentless drive for victimization is a misplaced understanding of compassion—a term now officially hijacked to serve the interests of income redistribution and an overly intrusive welfare state. There is no need to revisit old ground here, but my point concerns the consistent hijacking of a positive human emotion for destructive purposes.

(7) **We recognize taxes are essential but reject the notion that one should pay half of one's income to government.** Many contemporary commentators on the right have pressed the notion that no American should be forced to meet his maker and the tax collector on the same day. Another equally compelling thought: confiscatory marginal tax rates diminish productivity and they represent a terribly inefficient way to transfer wealth in a free

society, despite the protestations of class warriors past, present, and future.

(8) **We are pro-worker, while "working families" is in the eye of the beholder.** Whoever first coined the phrase "working families" deserves an honored place in the labor-left hall of fame. The slogan has been used to great effect by Democratic candidates since the New Deal. Rarely is the offender asked to define the phrase. This lack of definition is quite helpful for class warfare demagogues; class envy is a powerful strategy since few outside the true upper class believe themselves to be "rich." Accordingly, few middle- and upper-middle-class wage earners understand that *they* are the object of scorn from the class warriors of the left.

It is vital for the practitioners of this art to keep this dirty little secret quiet. Otherwise, imagine the shock directed their way once a fifty-four-thousand-dollar-a-year police sergeant and his fifty-thousand-dollar-a-year nurse wife discover that their joint income has not only made them "wealthy" but also the subject of great contempt from a certain set of politicians!

Of course, there are some (for example, see the Obama contribution lists from California and New York) who possess real wealth and still engage in class warfare rhetoric.

They are pro-worker but do not live in working-class neighborhoods. They are pro-teachers' union but send their children to elite private schools. They support tax increases yet employ an army of accountants to shield their bank accounts. They support gun control—until *their* community is threatened with violence. They bemoan Wall Street greed while they attend to their jobs—on Wall Street. They trumpet the merits of Obamacare, only to quietly seek "waivers" from its punishing mandates They are a perplexing bunch; their familiarity with working families is more apt to describe their domestic help than their peers and colleagues.

(9) **We know access to the courts is fundamental in a free society, but nobody has a constitutional right to sue you simply because you have insurance or deep pockets.** The notion that deep-pocket defendants who have done no wrong nor been negligent in their actions should pay an injured party simply because the defendant has money is unfair. Unfortunately, an oversupply of lawyers and

effective advertising from an aggressive plaintiffs bar has encouraged the notion that "somebody has to pay." The "gotta quarter, gotta lawyer" mentality leads to the troublesome thought process whereby any real or perceived harm must necessarily lead to a lawsuit, or at the very least, to an exchange of money. Of course, this overly litigious attitude serves to diminish the critical role attorneys play in a culture that values open access to the courts and legal redress for truly injured parties. Similarly, it can enhance an understandable attitude of skepticism and cynicism from a general public increasingly wary of an overburdened and expensive legal system.

(10) **We believe the notion of personal responsibility is the primary bulwark against the historical shift toward an ever-larger welfare state.** Although I did not invent it, I have repeated the "bothersome because it's true" line that the only difference between congressional Republicans and Democrats is that the Republicans support "Big Government" and Democrats support "Really Big Government." Any observer familiar with recent spending practices of the GOP-controlled Congress or the historic spending practices of the Obama-Reid-Pelosi era will quickly understand the accuracy of the charge. As a former member of Congress, I have experienced how easy it is to approve new spending measures, particularly when they are sold as benefiting "at risk" or marginal beneficiaries. The thousands of interest groups sponsoring member visits to Capitol Hill every year typically show up to ask for *more*, not less. Taken independently, it is easy to support these spending requests since the purpose or cause is generally positive in nature, and, in most cases, of benefit to the public image of the member. The problem occurs when the thousands of individual approvals are added together to generate yearly appropriations bills—a seemingly out-of-control process guaranteeing ever-larger government and ever-more-powerful constituencies interested in the perpetuation of undisciplined spending. It will take unprecedented fiscal discipline to combat this bipartisan spending binge—even with a seemingly reinvigorated House GOP Conference eager to restore fiscal prudence on Capitol Hill. A more consistent dialogue regarding the importance of personal responsibility in a free society would be of enormous benefit. Unfortunately, the promise of something for nothing carries with it a far more, albeit temporary,

attraction. These core, conflicting views (more personal responsibility versus more government responsibility) apply to just about every spending-related debate in our state capitols, as well as Capitol Hill. Here's hoping we reverse course from our present path. If not, the specter of an ever-expanding (and expensive) social welfare state crowding out individual initiative will be our unfortunate future.

(11) **We firmly believe that the contemporary decline of the family should be reversed, not accommodated.** An often-used but seldom-analyzed observation seems to be that because American society suffers from a high divorce rate, increasing numbers of single-parent families, and other "nontraditional" family relationships, it is somehow wrong to view traditional marriage and the nuclear family as a model or preferred option for young couples today. Well, not only is it the right thing to do, but it is important to defend it *now*, before Hollywood and pop culture degrade it to such an extent it can no longer be saved. In doing so, we again must be extraordinarily careful in making rational points and defining terms. *We do not claim that nontraditional relationships are unable to produce loving, functional families.* We do believe, however, that human history has shown the traditional family to be the most successful model for the rearing of children, and that children deserve and prosper from a strong male and female presence in their lives. Traditional marriages also serve as the best protection against rampant dependency and dysfunctional young adults.

Scientific literature reflects what then Senator Daniel Patrick Moynihan (D-NY), President Bill Clinton, Vice President Dan Quayle, Bill Cosby, and countless others have articulated: children raised in single-parent households begin life with two strikes against them. Among the more egregious consequences of fatherless households:

- Children in father-absent homes are five times more likely to be poor. In 2002, 7.8 percent of children in married-couple families were living in poverty, compared to 38.4 percent of children in female-householder families.[5]

---

[5] Jason Fields, "Children's Living Arrangements and Characteristics: March 2002," *Current Population Reports*, P20–547 (Washington, D.C.: U.S Census Bureau, 2003), Table C8.

- Almost 75 percent of American children living in single-parent families will experience poverty before they turn eleven years old. Only 20 percent of children in two-parent families will do the same.[6]
- During the year before their babies were born, 43 percent of unmarried mothers received welfare or food stamps, 21 percent received some type of housing subsidy, and 9 percent received another type of government transfer, such as unemployment insurance. For women who have another child, the proportion who receive welfare or food stamps rises to 53 percent.[7]
- Young men who grow up in homes without fathers are twice as likely to end up in jail as those who come from traditional two-parent families.[8]
- Seventy percent of juveniles in state-operated institutions come from fatherless homes.[9]

Some possess the brains, intellect, and willingness to overcome economic deprivation and thrive. Good for them. They are rightfully celebrated as accomplished individuals who overcame daunting obstacles. Many, however, do not thrive. They are more apt to join the ranks of the multigenerational poverty-stricken, those who repeat the cycle in their own lives. Why, then, would any culture celebrate such dysfunction? Why would anyone seek to identify such a difficult environment as equal to that of the traditional two-parent family?

The evidence on this point is indeed overwhelming, but when did we begin to require scientific literature to support such a commonsense proposition?

(12) We demand ethical behavior by public officials but do not expect perfection in any person or candidate. Repeated GOP sex

---

[6] *Just the Facts: A Summary of Recent information on America's Children and Their Families* (Washington, D.C.: National Commission on Children, 1993), 6.

[7] Christina Norland Audigier, Marcia Carlson, Irwin Garfinkel, Sara McLanahan, Nancy Reichman, and Julien Teitler, *The Fragile Families and Child Well-being Study: Baseline National Report* (Princeton, NJ: Bendheim-Thoman Center for Research on Child Well-being, 2003), 13.

[8] Cynthia Harper and Sara S. McLanahan, "Father Absence and Youth Incarceration," *Journal of Research on Adolescence* 14(3) (September 2004): 369–97.

[9] U.S. Department of Justice, Special Report, September 1988.

and money scandals have put to rest any thought about the GOP owning the high ground on congressional ethics. Truth be told, both parties will always have a member or two, or three, with a distorted view of ethics and ethical public behavior. This truth should not dissuade any citizen from the expectation that his or her representative will act in an ethical way. The standard here is not a difficult one, as most—but not all—ethical questions presented to a public official are fairly clear-cut in nature. A few, however, are truly close calls, and may require professional advice from ethics officers, personal soul-searching, and a hefty bit of common sense. Nonetheless, the people have the right to expect proper and ethical decisions from their representatives, even when such decisions mean less income, influence, prestige, or public support.

Governor Ehrlich speaks at one of many informal press conferences in front of the Historic State House in Annapolis.

Taking On
the Media Machine

*"If you don't read the newspapers, you are uninformed. If
you do read the newspapers, you are misinformed."*

—Mark Twain

MY MOST SEARING CONTEST with the media elite came in the
fall of 2004, when my decision to take on a veteran reporter erupted
into an unexpected high-stakes constitutional battle over freedom of
the press.

The story broke during an economic development mission to Asia
in October 2004. David Nitkin, a well-respected reporter for *The
Baltimore Sun*, wrote a series of stories charging that my administration was perpetrating a "secret land deal" in which the state was
intending to sell roughly eight hundred acres of land to a "politically
connected developer" from Baltimore.

The headlines were a case study in facts misrepresented, none more so than the October 20, 2004, attention-grabber, "Ehrlich OK'd deal for land." In reality, a "deal" had not been finalized. The proposal had to be approved by the transparent Board of Public Works (made up of the governor, treasurer, and comptroller) meeting in *open* session, and I had told my general services secretary that it was "worth pursuing"—not exactly a final approval, or even an "Okay."

Further, the "politically connected developer" supposedly set to profit from the land swap was a major fund-raiser...for the *Democratic* Party, a fact that did appear in the middle of the story. The man in question, a well-respected contractor and philanthropist named Willard Hackerman, had, to that point, never given me a penny in campaign contributions, supported my opponent in the 2002 gubernatorial campaign, and had been closely allied with my strongest critics in the Maryland legislature!

Perhaps worse, four weeks later, *The Sun* ran a front-page graphic intending to show how much state-owned land my administration was considering selling to help resolve a state budget deficit. Remarkably, the graphic depicted much of the state park system in Maryland as being up for sale. A reader of *The Sun* that morning would have thought I was attempting to sell approximately one-tenth of the state's landmass to developers. One-tenth! Needless to say, the graphic was outrageous and inaccurate. After irate calls from my communications office, *The Sun* ran a watered-down "clarification," to the effect that I could not have unilaterally authorized final approval of any land sale, *inside* the paper the next day, where few readers would see it. With regard to the inaccurate front-page map of preserved state lands, a correction and apology was issued the next day. Alas, the damage was already done.

Damage Control and Its Aftermath

My personal attempts to reason with Nitkin, as well as the daily attempts of my press staff, were unsuccessful. Facts to the contrary notwithstanding, the story line was not about to change. So, we took action. On my instruction, my press office directed the administration's agency-based public information officers to cease answering

Nitkin's questions *and* those of Michael Olesker, a liberal *Sun* opinion columnist who regularly took batting practice on Republicans in general and my administration in particular.

The Sun's leadership went apoplectic, filing suit in federal district court, claiming their constitutional rights had been violated, and stating that I "had set a dangerous precedent for all…citizens." They charged that by choosing to no longer speak with journalists who had been chronically negligent in their news coverage of my administration, I had somehow flouted the First Amendment to the U.S. Constitution.

"This is really highly unusual," said Robert H. Giles, former president of the *American Society of Newspaper Editors*, in a *Sun* story.[10] "The governor may be trying to change the people on the beat or [intimidate] the columnist.…It is not the responsibility of the governor to take matters into his hands and influence the selection of journalists covering stories.'

As *The Sun's* publisher wrote in an open letter to readers, "No governor, Republican or Democrat, should be allowed to pick and choose whom state employees speak to based on whether the governor approves of their views Left unchallenged, Gov. Ehrlich could prevent any citizen with whom he disagrees from gaining access to information from taxpayer-paid state government employees."[11]

In other words, I should have no power over the actions of press officers appointed by me to serve my administration. Another salient fact would prove quite helpful in court: *The Sun's* other reporters and columnists enjoyed daily access to me and other administration spokesmen, a fact unreported by the newspaper.

The Sun was not alone in its crusade. The Associated Press, *The Washington Post*, and other major news organizations joined in public condemnation of my actions. The story took off, dominating radio and television airwaves in Maryland and generating legal and political scrutiny across the country. Suddenly, major news organizations across the country wanted me to explain and justify my decision to impose this press "ban."

---

[10] Greg Barrett and Stephanie Hanes, "Sun Files Suit to Lift Ban on Journalists by Ehrlich," *The Baltimore Sun*, December 4, 2004.

[11] Ibid.

From Baltimore to Albuquerque, newspapers expressed outrage with my decision. Law experts around the country weighed in, albeit on both sides of the issue. Abraham Dash, a law professor at the University of Maryland, opined: "The Supreme Court has said over and over that there's no duty for the government to give out information."[12] Dash concluded that I "probably" had the right to instruct my employees as to how they dealt with the press.

Another constitutional law professor, David C. Vladeck of Georgetown University, disagreed, telling *The Sun*: "I think that the ban itself is unconstitutional because the ban is too broad....What I'm concerned about is that the governor has pushed this issue in a way that almost necessitates a visit to the courts. I would hope that cooler heads will prevail soon."[13]

Even conservative radio hosts and Republican opinion leaders in Maryland expressed their uneasiness with my edict, albeit for more political reasons. At the very least, they believed I had committed a major public relations blunder by picking a fight with already hostile opponents who buy ink by the proverbial barrel and who were ready, willing, and able to sustain a long-term legal battle over such a fundamental issue. Some members of my senior staff agreed; they feared a public backlash with the charge that I had become too thin-skinned to lead. Still, my gut told me more people than not respected my decision to take a stand against factually incorrect reporting. My inclination received further support when even Democratic members of the General Assembly would make a point to pull me aside to offer congratulations on my refusal to back down once the court challenges began.

By taking on *The Sun* and, by extension, the media establishment, I found myself in a position few, if any, public servants would envy: every reporter covering this high-stakes story had a vested, professional interest in my failure. If I were to prevail in court, the precedent for limiting a journalist's perceived limitless powers and access would be reaffirmed in a substantive way. The wide-ranging repercussions of this case were lost on no one.

---

[12] "The Sun Sues Maryland Governor," Newsmax.com, December 6, 2004.

[13] Matthew Dolan, "Legal Experts Divided on Ehrlich Ban Affecting 2 Sun Writers," *The Baltimore Sun*, December 7, 2004.

Round One went to us in a knockout, as Judge William D. Quarles Jr. of the U.S. District Court of Maryland found *The Sun's* suit to be "without merit."

"*The Sun* seeks a privileged status beyond that of the private citizen," Quarles wrote. "*The Sun* seeks the declaration of a constitutional right that neither the Supreme Court nor the 4th Circuit has recognized—and, in fact, seeks more access than that accorded a private citizen."[14]

Our public relations strategy was straightforward. After the initial case filing and Quarles' opinion, we went straight to talk radio and television to make a central point: this was not a case of my political interests versus a newspaper's interests; this was about a newspaper's interests versus a reader's interests. In other words, the average *Sun* reader deserves to know the content presented on the news pages, as opposed to the editorial pages, is based in *fact*. The reader also deserves to know the contents of an opinion column are neither fabricated nor outright plagiarized. *The Sun* had failed in both respects, and I was placing my reputation and plenty of political capital on the line to hold the newspaper accountable.

After months of mostly negative reaction from around the country, a Fourth Circuit Court of Appeals panel of judges upheld the lower court's ruling. After two bitter losses in the courts, *The Sun* declined a further appeal to the full Fourth Circuit. The so-called ban stayed in place for the remainder of my time in office.

Read Between the Lines

An interesting sidebar to the inclusion of veteran *Sun* opinion columnist Michael Olesker in our press ban should be noted. Less than a year after the court ruled in my favor, Olesker resigned after a long internal *Sun* investigation uncovered evidence of plagiarism in his work.

The Sun's January 4, 2006, edition noted numerous instances in which Olesker had apparently appropriated work of reporters from *The Sun*, *The New York Times*, and *The Washington Post*.

---

[14] Stephen Kiehl, "Sun's Challenge of Ehrlich Order Is Dismissed by a Federal Judge," *The Baltimore Sun*, February 15, 2005.

In fact, I had not intended for Olesker to be a part of my original edict. That add-on was the product of my communications director, Paul Schurick. Why? A November 16, 2004, Olesker opinion piece had contained a description of Schurick during a press availability "struggling mightily to keep a straight face."[15] The only problem with the description was that Olesker had not been present during the press conference. When my staff complained about Olesker's unprofessionalism (it is impossible to ascribe a facial expression when the reporter was not present to witness it), he admitted his mistake and apologized, sort of, by claiming his description was meant "metaphorically," not "literally," according to *The Sun*.

Olesker could not, however, overcome a subsequent series of plagiarism-related allegations researched by Gadi Dechter, then a reporter at the *Baltimore City Paper*, and his assistant Anne Howard, who discovered "several instances" (according to *The Sun*) in which Olesker appeared to misappropriate work from other journalists.

It is possible to infer our ban and the subsequent lawsuit contributed to the resignation. Olesker himself seems to believe it to be so, as reflected in his comments to *Sun* reporter Nick Madigan on his last day:

"I made mistakes. . . . I would never take somebody else's work and call it my own. I have always tried to serve my readers as honorably as possible. In the current climate, with so many political eyes staring at me and this newspaper, I feel it's in everyone's best interest for me to resign."[16]

Once news of the resignation hit, the press rushed to my office for comment, hoping for an "I-told-you-so" response from an empowered governor. Instead, they received a "no comment." I took no joy in the columnist's departure, despite his unremitting negative attacks on all things Ehrlich. In fact, when I was subsequently asked by a potential employer whether I had a problem with Olesker being hired, I declined to intervene.

---

[15] Paul Moore, "Weighing the Merits of Ehrlich Complaints," *The Baltimore Sun*, April 21, 2005.

[16] Nick Madigan, "Longtime Sun Columnist Olesker Resigns," *The Baltimore Sun*, January 4, 2006.

I had not contested any reporter's right to conduct attack operations under the cloak of freedom of the press—such a position would have been small-minded and unconstitutional. On the other hand, reporters have never enjoyed a right to unfettered access to anyone, let alone a public official. Neither have they been given the right to make up news stories or invent descriptions of events without challenge. Even when such blunders are acknowledged, readers have a right to expect better than a day-old retraction buried at the bottom of Page B2. The bottom line is that the public has a right to form opinions grounded in fact, a right too easily lost when mere allegations are dressed up as fact for the sake of selling newspapers, or to strengthen a particular newspaper's political agenda.

In the interest of full disclosure, it could be that I was given a bit too much credit by my supporters and anti-*Sun* pundits for my controversial stance in *The Sun* litigation. Truth be told, I wonder whether I would have been so aggressive against a newspaper with a better reputation; would I have possessed the guts to "ice" a reporter from *The Washington Post* or *The New York Times*? The question is impossible to answer, but there is little doubt in my mind that the preexisting bitter relationship with *The Sun* editorial board and its reputation as a second-tier daily (a far cry from its once-lofty perch as one of America's top newspapers) made the initial decision much easier than a casual observer might believe.

Encountering More Criticism

Parenthetically, and not surprisingly, the relentless criticism from *The Sun*'s editorial pages maintained itself throughout the run-up to the 2006 election. According to Professor Richard Vatz of Towson University, during the *entire* 2006 gubernatorial campaign, there was not one piece favorable to me by name on its op-ed page, a page traditionally open to opposing views. Moreover, the paper sported as its only op-ed page columnist focused on Maryland issues an inveterate liberal who consistently criticized my administration.

The Sun's tarnished credibility also made it easier to withstand sharp attacks from more credible news organizations around the country. Even during the most difficult days, with my Office of Legal

Counsel literally begging me to settle the lawsuit, I believed we continued to enjoy a more-than-respectable level of credibility with the people—the ultimate arbiters.

This incident demonstrated the level of journalistic hostility public officials often face and the lengths to which our team was willing to fight an entrenched media establishment. It was not a particularly enjoyable experience, especially given the public and private criticisms from those who agreed with the substance of the decision but thought my refusal to back down was a poor political move that would come back to haunt us. Nevertheless, I believed then—and continue to believe—that it would distinguish our team as principled players ready, willing, and able to fight for positions we believed in, even when doing so would be uncomfortable in the short term, or potentially damaging to my political ambitions in the long term.

Taking On
the Multicultural Police

"In the first place, we should insist that if the immigrant who comes here does in good faith become an American and assimilates himself to us, he shall be treated on an exact equality with everyone else, for it is an outrage to discriminate against any such man because of creed, or birthplace, or origin. But this is predicated upon the man's becoming in very fact an American and nothing but an American.... There can be no divided allegiance here.... We have room for but one flag, the American flag... We have room for but one language here, and that is the English language... and we have room for but one, soul [sic] loyalty and that loyalty is to the American people."

—THEODORE ROOSEVELT, 1919

THE RON SMITH SHOW is a popular talk radio show, well established in the Baltimore metropolitan market. The host is bright, with a dry personality and a decidedly anti-authority bent. Ratings are strong, befitting the fifty-thousand-watt reach of its mothership, WBAL radio.

Periodic appearances on talk radio are not unusual for modern-day politicians, particularly GOP officeholders. In many districts around the country, talk radio is the preferred format to combat the bias of traditionally liberal metropolitan daily newspapers. Early on, I decided to maximize the use of radio to contest our opponents at *The Baltimore Sun* and *The Washington Post* (although *The Post* did endorse my reelection bid in 2006), who never quite got over the shock of my election on November 5, 2002.

At that time, *The Ron Smith Show* attracted up to fifty thousand listeners in drive time between 5 and 6 P.M. My practice was to call in between 5:30 and 6 P.M. to comment on the hot topics of the day, knowing it was an opportunity to answer attacks from the opposition or make points of my own. One of my appearances would prove most newsworthy, although it was neither planned nor the first time I had expressed this particular opinion.

"This" view was my response to a man who had called about controversial remarks made that day by then Democratic State Comptroller William Donald Schaefer, the former governor, Baltimore mayor, and political icon who was known to express independent, politically incorrect opinions from time to time. Schaefer was larger than life. As Baltimore's mayor in the 1980s, he earned praise as the Best Big City Mayor in America.[17] In keeping with his showman's persona, and in order to generate favorable publicity for the newly constructed Baltimore aquarium in 1981, Schaefer famously donned a 1920s-era swimsuit and plunged into the aquarium's new seal pool to the delight (not to mention the surprise) of astonished members of the press and public—and probably the seals as well. His victory margins in his two races for governor were 64 percent and 20 percent, respectively. He cherished his reputation as a free and fierce thinker, from his well-known propensity to respond to nasty constituent letters with even nastier responses (and on rare occasions, show up at the constituent's doorstep with his nasty response in hand) to a well-publicized, last-minute endorsement of Republican George H.W.

---

[17] Richard Ben Cramer, "Can the Best Mayor Win?" *Esquire*, October 1984.

Bush in 1992. The last incident set off alarm bells in Democratic precincts around the country. A few in the Maryland Democratic Party
would never forget nor forgive this particular indiscretion. No big
deal for Schaefer, however. He simply had no patience for phonies or
those who lacked trustworthiness. Bush passed that litmus test; Bill
Clinton failed.

As a matter of practice, however, the periodic dustups from a
Schaefer utterance or episode would typically prove to be brief.

On this occasion, as a result of a frustrating experience at a local
McDonald's with an "English-challenged" employee, Schaefer had
lamented what he perceived as the inability or unwillingness of a
growing number of immigrants to learn the English language. The
caller asked for my thoughts on the subject. Speaking on the phone
from my office in the Maryland State House, I answered as follows:

> With regard to this culture, English is the language. Can [immi-
> grants] obviously honor their ethnic traditions and languages at
> home and other places? Of course. They are not mutually exclu-
> sive. The point here is there is a major distinction between ethnic
> pride, which is appropriate, and multiculturalism, which is dam-
> aging to the society in my view. I reject the idea of multicultural-
> ism. To the extent that [a] melting pot becomes one culture to
> celebrate ethnicity—wonderful. But once you get into this multi-
> cultural crap, this bunk, you run into a problem.[18]

I went on to the next caller without a worry as to potential repercussions. Why should I have been concerned? After all, in Congress
I regularly delivered speeches in public forums on the benefits of a
multi*ethnic* melting pot society in contrast to the dangers of a divided,
multi*cultural* nation. Never before had my comments on the subject
incited controversy. In fact, to the extent I was concerned at all about
my remarks, it was my use of the word "crap" that gave me second
thoughts. After the show, I recall thinking the use of the word was inappropriate on the airwaves, but even stronger language could have
been employed to describe what I viewed as a dangerous, destructive

---

[18] Bob Ehrlich, radio interview by Ron Smith, *The Ron Smith Show*, WBAL-AM, May 6, 2004.

movement within our culture. The slang term I had thrown out was to stem my rising anger; the politically correct left had indeed made progress in its long-running campaign to immunize multiculturalism from critical analysis and criticism.

The reaction from the left was immediate and strikingly antagonistic. The Washington Post editorial board was initially critical, but The Sun went so far as to publish an editorial criticizing my comments entirely in Spanish. If the left's goal was to show how out of touch I was with its brave new world of open borders and unconditional tolerance, then it succeeded. Newspapers across the country added their own liberal outrage. I realized what a chord I had struck when the Hispanic social activist group CASA of Maryland started picketing my public appearances around the state.

The outrage didn't end there. The Montgomery County Council approved a resolution calling on me to apologize. The mayor of Baltimore denounced my remarks in Spanish. In Takoma Park, a liberal enclave on the outskirts of Washington, D.C., a group of local Latino leaders and approximately fifty immigrant advocates gathered to denounce my comments. Later, Montgomery County and Baltimore leaders gathered to criticize me—in English, Spanish, and Korean.

"This is an attack, an attack on our humanity, on our communities," said state delegate Ana Sol Gutierrez.[19]

Another liberal state lawmaker compared me to Archie Bunker. One disgruntled Hispanic activist made the expected comparison to Adolf Hitler (more on him later), Joe McCarthy, George Wallace, and the perpetrators of lynching—all in one letter.

Of course, the polar opposite reaction occurred on the right, as talk radio hosts, particularly Smith, praised my "courage" for standing up to the PC crowd on one of its primary issues.

The Washington Post quoted a retired Air Force officer, Chief Master Sgt. Ken Witkin, as saying, "I spent thirty years in the Air Force fighting communism. I gave up thirty years of my life, and

---

[19] Jeff Barker and Tom Pelton, "O'Malley Rebuts 'English' Remarks," The Baltimore Sun, May 12, 2004.

I didn't give it up so I could start learning Spanish....Every single veteran I've talked to feels the same way."[20]

Others battled more over the proper definition of multiculturalism than my actual statements. *The Washington Post* editorialized:

> [T]he trouble with multiculturalism is that the word means different things to different people. To some it implies a radical departure from traditional systems of integrating foreigners into this country, a refusal to teach children American history and the enshrinement of Spanish as a de facto official language. To others it just means tolerance. From the published excerpts of Mr. Ehrlich's radio interview, it seems he thought he was denouncing multiculturalism in the former sense, but he made it sound as if he was denouncing multiculturalism in the latter sense.[21]

At least *The Post* got it half correct.

While my statement was not intended to incite, it was a shot across the bow of an increasingly intolerant liberal establishment. It also bolstered the notion that some in elective office are willing to engage the PC police and not back down when the kitchen gets hot. In fact, I was given dozens of opportunities by reporters, supporters, critics, and others to back down and apologize for my comments about multiculturalism but I steadfastly refused. As the firestorm died down several days later, a Washington-area radio host asked me how much political damage I thought would result from my comments. "I don't care," I answered. "The honest answer is very little. I was not elected to be politically correct. I was not elected to be safe."[22]

Don't Back Down

Refusing to back down and then reasserting your controversial views when confronted with PC-derived moral outrage is the winning strategy in today's culture wars. Voters must believe their elected

---

[20] Darragh Johnson, Matthew Mosk, "Immigrant Remarks by Ehrlich Still Burn," *The Washington Post*, May 12, 2004.

[21] Editorial, "Un Big Mac, Por Favor," *The Washington Post*, May 13, 2004.

[22] Robert Ehrlich, interview with Mark Plotkin, WTOP-AM.

representative possesses the courage of his or her convictions and will rely on the same when faced with extreme unpleasantness. On the left, there appears to be no room for debate on issues held near and dear. The repeated use of derisive language and disparaging context is the "go-to" strategy whenever and wherever leftist orthodoxy is violated.

So, the natural and very human tendency to back off when confronted with moral high ground indignation must be overcome. For me, the challenge was not so difficult in the aftermath of my multiculturalism remarks because the opinion expressed represented the commonsense view held by so many Marylanders (and Americans) once the issue is thought through to its logical conclusion.

I suspect there is more to the overreaction on the left than merely exposing one of its favorite issues. It is the fear of exposure to what the proponents of multiculturalism truly want that drives their emotionalism. If the actual goal of the multicultural crowd is acceptance of more than one cultural set of values within our society, and it's feared that such a goal would be rejected as dangerous if articulated, why not vent your rage at those who dare to expose the real foundation and goals of the movement? That way, it would be understood by all that those who dare challenge the real agenda of multiculturalists will be subject to scorn and ridicule. And how many public officials with something to lose are willing to put their image, poll numbers, or reputation in jeopardy for such a cause?

The NAME Game

An interesting side note to *The Ron Smith Show* incident occurred after the initial draft of this chapter was completed.

On October 30, 2007, Robert Holland of the Lexington Institute, a free market–oriented think tank in Arlington, Virginia, published an op-ed in *The Baltimore Sun* entitled, "Was Ehrlich right about multiculturalism?"

The article reviewed the half- and full-day workshops available at the seventeenth annual national convention of the National Association for Multicultural Education (NAME), the primary advocacy group for the teaching of multiculturalism. Available workshops included the following:

- "The Unbearable Whiteness of Being: Dismantling White Privilege and Supporting Anti-Racist Education in Our Classrooms and Schools." Taught by a professor from St. Cloud State University in Minnesota, this session "is designed to help educators identify and deconstruct their own white privilege and in so doing more deeply commit themselves to anti-racist teaching and critical multicultural teaching."
- "Talking About Religious Oppression and Unpacking Christian Privilege." This session, taught by a team of professors, "will examine the dynamics of Christian privilege and oppression of minority religious groups and nonbelievers as constructed and maintained on three distinct levels: individual, institutional, and societal. A historical and legal lecturette will be presented and participants will engage in interactive learning modules."
- "Beyond Celebrating Diversity: Teaching Teachers How to be Critical Multicultural Educators." Taught by NAME regional director Paul Gorski, founder of the activist group EdChange, this session will start from the premise that multiculturalism's greatest danger "comes from educators who ostensibly support its goals, but whose work—cultural plunges, food fairs, etc.— reflects a compassionate conservative consciousness rather than social justice. This session focuses on preparing teachers, not for celebrating diversity, but for achieving justice in schools and society."[23]

Holland's piece noted that school board members ought to pay special attention to the foregoing subject matter since they approve the expenditure of taxpayers' money for kindergarten through twelfth-grade teachers to attend the NAME convention.

In view of the wholesale silliness represented by these wacky PC police, one wonders where the taxpayers can turn in order to secure

---

[23] Robert Holland, "Was Ehrlich Right about Multiculturalism?" *The Baltimore Sun*, October 30, 2007.

a refund. One can only hope that exposure of this organization and its teaching goals and methods will one day lead to so much ridicule that the entire concept will become a mere relic of a failed intellectual endeavor. At least, let's hope so.

Multiculturalism Down Under

In the course of performing research for this book, I had the opportunity to review similar instances in which a commonly accepted view of culture, nationhood, and assimilation became the subject of major public debate and where the proponents of the politically incorrect remarks stuck to principles rather than indulge an outraged PC crowd in its relentless campaign of intimidation and threats.

One of the more well-known examples took place in Australia during the fall of 2006. The series of events that followed remarks on multiculturalism by John Howard, then prime minister of Australia, were remarkably similar to what transpired in the aftermath of my remarks around the same time frame.

First, the actual words and commonsense views expressed by the prime minister on the topic of Muslim integration, with particular emphasis on the *positive* contributions of Islamic communities on the Australian culture:

Australia has been greatly enriched by immigration and most people who have come to this nation have happily integrated with the community...They have willingly embraced the Australian way of life. They have become part of the fabric of the nation and have helped make Australia the great country it is today. I have said many times that people who come to this country—no matter where they are from—should become part of the Australian community...There are small sections of some communities, including the Islamic community, that are resistant to integration. As I have said on many occasions, 99 per cent [sic] of the Islamic community of Australia has integrated into, and is part of, the Australian community. They have added great value to our society and are making a valuable contribution to the nation. Australia's Islamic community is also worried about this tiny minority. Most of the Islamic people I know are as appalled as me by the failure of some within the community to integrate. It is up to all of us to try to overcome the resistance.[24]

Fiery reactions from multicultural apologists, with the usual xenophobic charges, characterized the left's response: "Howard plays the race card," read one September 22, 2006, *Canberra Times* headline.

"We are in a different era in which the leader of this country, for the first time in much more than half a century, is promoting a xenophobia which divides the country and which harms citizens in this country who have no right to be picked out by a leader for special criticism in the way that John Howard has," said one Australian politician.[25]

Finally, after incessant media coverage and speculation around the issue of an expected apology, there arose a series of definite reaffirmations by Prime Minister Howard. In one instance, in response to reporters' questions, the reaffirmation was merely a commonsense restatement about the central importance of a baseline common culture in a multiethnic society: "I think they are missing the point and the point is that I don't care and Australian people don't care where people come from. . . . There's a small section of the Islamic community which is unwilling to integrate and I have said generally all migrants . . . they have to integrate."[26]

Again, "no apology provided" sends a profound message of courage and willingness to stand up on principle to the culture warriors of the multicultural left. Moreover, a strong reaffirmation often leads to a quick end to the media circus as the press begins to accept, if not fully understand, that no "mea culpa" is forthcoming, and the views and definitions expressed are so clearly the majority opinion that there is not much else to write or opine about.

---

[24] John Howard, "It's Sense, Not Discrimination," *Daily Telegraph* (Sydney), September 2, 2006.

[25] "Howard Australia's Most Xenophobic Leader, Greens Say," ABC News, September 2, 2006.

[26] Richard Kerbaj, "Australia: Howard Stands by Muslim Integration," *The Muslim News*, January 9, 2007.

The Port of Baltimore Case

Yet, every rule has its exception. Indeed, there are instances where the PC police will abandon its moral outrage in a heartbeat in order to score temporary political points.

I was at the center of such a case in 2006. That winter, members of Congress and interest groups on the left and right began complaining about a business deal that would have placed a company controlled by the United Arab Emirates in charge of certain operations at several U.S. ports, including the Port of Baltimore. Per the negotiated deal, Dubai Ports World would have acquired London-based Peninsular & Oriental Steam Navigation Co. (P&O) for a reported $6.8 billion. P&O regulates container operations at two publicly owned marine terminals in Baltimore. The deal would have provided UAE-owned Dubai Ports World port operations in New York, Newark, New Jersey, Philadelphia, Miami, and New Orleans.

Despite the fact that the deal pertained to only terminal operations (mostly managing the flow of container cargo) and that foreign companies have operated in American ports for decades, opponents unleashed a volley of xenophobic, anti-Arab demagoguery.

"Not so long as I'm mayor and not so long as I have breath in my body," said Baltimore Mayor Martin O'Malley. "We are not going to turn over the port of Baltimore to a foreign government. It's not going to happen."[27]

Few commentators bothered to point out that the proposed deal did not constitute the "turning over" of anything to a foreign government, let alone operations at such a busy port.

"In a post-9/11 world, we cannot afford to surrender our port operations to foreign governments," then Senator Hillary Clinton (D-NY) said. "Port security is national security and national security is port security."[28]

---

[27] Meredith Cohn and Gwyneth K. Shaw, "Ehrlich Objects to Port Deal," *The Baltimore Sun*, February 21, 2006.

[28] Bill Van Auken, "The Clintons, the Doles and the Dubai Port Deal: Political Duplicity and Class Interest," World Socialist Website, March 4, 2006, www.wsws.org/articles/2006/mar2006/duba-m04.shtml.

Little notice was devoted to the split in the Clinton household. At the same time Hillary Clinton was denouncing the proposed ports agreement in the U.S. Senate, her husband was advising the UAE on how to secure Washington's approval. He also pocketed $450,000 for a speech in Dubai, and took donations of up to $1 million for the Clinton presidential library from the UAE. Even more intriguing was the president's suggestion to the Dubai royal family to hire his former press secretary, Joe Lockhart, to help push the ports deal through.

To be fair, reaction from the right was mixed, as the proposed deal led to sniping from conservative commentators and congressional Republicans. But it was the fierce opposition from the left that was so striking at the time. The Dubai Ports episode showed how selectively indignant the left can be, depending on the target and the stakes involved. In this instance, the opportunity to hammer President Bush on a core Republican issue (security) was strong enough to outweigh the xenophobic profiling of an Arab country—even an Arab country allied with the West in the War on Terror. I often refer back to this incident whenever I see a liberal politician bemoaning America's diminished prestige in the Arab world. There are many reasons for our poor reputation on the Arab street, but why is it that nobody sees this shameful incident as at least contributing to American public relations problems? Does anybody on the left take any measure of responsibility for the wholesale vilification of one of our few Arab allies in the War on Terror? Most assuredly, the Dubai Ports deal reflected a type of situational intolerance that would appear to be at odds with the worldview of the PC crowd—if that same PC crowd were consistent in its approach to ethnic issues. Alas, it most certainly is not!

The Great Melting Pot

A number of observations emerge from these recent experiences with culture and ethnicity. First, it is important to remember that just about everything we value in America has a distinctly American label attached to it, from common political principles to common social values to a common language. For generations, we were taught about the power of assimilation, of a melting pot made from diverse ethnic backgrounds brought together in a common quest to develop a common bond in order to strengthen a common culture. In the case of my multiculturalism comments, I could not help but be amused by the spectacle of ethnic special-interest group protests against an administration whose job description included the empowerment of recent immigrants through assimilation programs such as "English as a Second Language" classes and entrepreneurial studies. In fact, the primary task of ethnic commissions at the state and federal levels is to assimilate people of diverse cultures into one culture—a uniquely American culture—made up of unparalleled democratic political values, equality, capitalism, a common language, religious freedom, and federalism. Baseball and apple pie, too.

In neither incident retold on the previous pages did the language police secure the victory they wanted. In the case of my *Ron Smith Show* comments, I would neither apologize nor back down. In fact, I took every public opportunity available to address the issue, to make the point that silence only strengthens the resolve of those who wish to remake our society into something it was never meant to be. The lesson? The commonsense majority must not back down when expressing or defending widely held commonsense attitudes, particularly when done to the dismay of the PC police and its intolerant and increasingly out-of-touch friends in the media.

Taking On Economic Guilt Trips

"I hope gas prices go as high as they have to go to get the rest of these morons off the road in these big Hummers."

—CNN ANCHOR JACK CAFFERTY
(March 26, 2006, on CNN's *In the Money*)

MOST AMERICANS HAVE GREETED the arrival of the latest oil crisis with a mixture of anger and disgust: anger due to dramatic price increases at the gasoline pump, and disgust because our dependence on foreign sources of oil has only increased since the gas line days of the 1970s.

Conversely, many leaders on the left have experienced a difficult time containing their exuberance. This "celebration" of sky-high gas prices and significant increases in the cost of energy may strike some as rather odd; why does glee follow from $4.50 a gallon gas and crude oil hitting upwards of $125 a barrel? Why do left-leaning academics and politicians take pleasure in such a dramatic hit on the U.S.

economy and an accompanying diminution in the standard of living for so many people? What happened to all that alleged concern for the plight of America's "working families"? Why would Nancy Pelosi and Harry Reid go to such great effort to avoid a real debate about energy policy in the House and Senate?

What may seem counterintuitive to many has not been such a great surprise to me. Insight into this attitude follows from four years of service on the House Banking and Financial Services Committee, where I was exposed to almost daily doses of class warfare ideology emanating from some of the most effective practitioners of this most divisive art form. On any particular day and pertaining to just about any finance-related issue, members such as Joe Kennedy (D-MA), Chuck Schumer (D-NY), Barney Frank (D-MA), Maxine Waters (D-CA), and Bernie Sanders (D-VT) would engage in an aggressive indictment of one or another aspect of market capitalism. They'd bemoan the failure of the Community Reinvestment Act to prevent redlining; it was daily lobbying aimed at pressuring banks to underwrite subprime mortgages in poor urban communities (more on this painful topic in Chapter 6, "Taking on the Mortgage Meltdown"). A common criticism centered on the alleged evils of tax cuts for "the rich" to the even greater moral sin of wealth disparity. It was daily batting practice born of very real and deep philosophical differences with the new Republican majority, with more than a bit of bitterness owing to their new and unexpected minority status in the House of Representatives.

Banks (as opposed to credit unions) were attacked as too detached from their local communities and too profit-driven; in fact, a popular indictment centered on the negatives associated with marketplace-driven profit. For a freshman Republican from a right-leaning Democratic district, it was an eye-opening experience. These were the *real* Democrats, and they were angry. Their unrelenting distrust of market capitalism made quite an impact on me.

It was from these freshman memories that I recognized a similar drumbeat during our more recent national energy debates, but with a far different tone from that of 1973. Today, the Organization of Petroleum Exporting Countries is demonized far less often than the American consumer's appetite for heavy vehicles. The theme of greedy American oil companies and a negligent American consumer is ripe with opportunity for profound cultural change. Here, finally, is an opportunity to accomplish so many "punch list" items on the new left's energy agenda: declaring war on the SUV, continuing to limit America's ability to develop domestic sources of oil (because we must stop feeding our oil "addiction"), ending dependence on fossil fuels—even curtailing American consumption and our standard of living (why should we enjoy the benefits of capitalism when a larger social welfare state could be so... egalitarian?).

The euphoria following this latest crisis in the energy markets leaves a few interested observers wondering about the real goal. A sampling of energy-related declarations from left-leaning journalists and politicians speaks volumes:

"Somehow we have to figure out how to boost the price of gasoline to the levels in Europe."[29]
— STEVEN CHU, PRESIDENT OBAMA'S SECRETARY OF ENERGY

"We are the worst polluter on the planet. We are 4 percent of the world's population, we're putting out 25 percent of the world's greenhouse gas. America's going to have to change!"
—SENATOR JOHN EDWARDS (D-NC)[30]

"[W]e definitely want to move beyond petroleum. And so there will be a supply side offered by the Democrats and it will include everything from battery technology to making sure that we have good home domestic supply, and looking... about moving faster on those kinds of things like wind and solar that can help us with our high cost of natural gas."[31]
—SENATOR MARIA CANTWELL (D-WA)

---

[29] Peter Ferrara, "Obama's War on Oil," *The American Spectator*, May 4, 2011.
[30] Brendan Farrington, "Edwards, Kucinich Woo Machinists Union," The Associated Press, August 28, 2007.
[31] Maria Cantwell, interview on *Money and Politics*, Bloomberg TV, July 21, 2008.

Possibly the most brazen example of the left's self-loathing regarding the modern American lifestyle and standard of living came from CBS reporter Bob Simon in 2002:

> If we were to really live well, and by that I mean: being less greedy, taking better care of our poor and our needy, and stop making impossible demands on our planet's resources, I think we would plunge our enemies into shame.[32]

Regarding the above, I have four observations.

Our Reliance on Foreign Oil

First, most Americans finally understand the dangerous economic and foreign policy consequences that follow an overreliance on foreign sources of oil. It has taken more than thirty years and three major oil crises to get us to understand how hostile regimes in the post-9/11 era can cause havoc on our economy; in fact, these regimes are more than happy to do so.

Fortunately, this new recognition has given rise to a wider acceptance of alternative sources of energy—wind, solar, hydrogen, and biofuels. The calls for additional diversification from these clean alternatives, with the exception of nuclear, have come from every corner of the ideological spectrum. Seems the new left shares the old left's distaste for greenhouse gas–free nuclear power plants—a view that will only become more pronounced in the aftermath of the 2011 nuclear power plant disaster in Japan.

Unfortunately, the new enthusiasm for alternatives has not extended to a call for additional supply for oil, natural gas, or coal production. Similarly, the lack of new energy infrastructure limits our ability to generate increased capacity in the short term, with a severely strained power grid as the unfortunate result. In more tangible terms, many energy analysts fear widespread, periodic brownouts will occur within the next three to five years, as even a tepid recovery

---

[32] Bob Simon, *60 Minutes*, September 8, 2002.

produces additional demand for energy. An extended recovery would only exacerbate demand and drive prices ever higher.

What to Do in the Interim

The second observation portends a more difficult, controversial debate: what to do *until* energy independence is achieved, and why so many left-leaning activists include sustained attacks against American prosperity as part of their campaign for energy independence.

The energy consumption guilt trip is typically phrased in rhetorical terms—why should unenlightened U.S. consumers be allowed to consume such a large percentage of the world's oil supplies when they compose only 3 percent of the world's population? It is a monumental economic guilt trip right out of any class warrior's agenda. On one level, the goal is rather easily achieved—playing to the heartstrings of a generous and prosperous people is well received in many quarters. The philanthropic nature of the American people is well documented. We *want* other countries to grow and prosper the way America has for 235 years. So, shouldn't we feel just a bit guilty for the way we live in our consumer- and consumption-driven society? And just think about how much more popular America could be if we could just pull back a bit on our lifestyles (more on this below).

Fortunately, this more significant goal is a harder sell. Indeed, it is my profound hope that it will prove to be an impossible sale. In rhetorical terms, it speaks to an economy of more limited goals and resources; of a marketplace of diminishing returns quite *unlike* American workers have come to expect over the past 235 years. In more tangible terms, it is about a general restructuring of our economy and standard of living. Gone would be the notion that each generation of American worker is expected to be more efficient and, as a result, achieve a higher standard of living than the previous generation. This new culture does not speak to an expansive opportunity society grounded in consumerism and wealth creation. It contemplates, seemingly with great enthusiasm, rationing and limits. It is anti-consumption. It advocates government-sponsored health care. It supports higher marginal tax rates. It seeks to expand Medicaid to middle-income households. Its foundation is an expanded social welfare state from cradle to grave. And, unless these circumstances are understood by the American electorate, it will be coming to a government near... *you*!

The view that American prosperity should be a source of cultural embarrassment is a hard sell to most Americans because it is counterintuitive to our opportunity-driven country. Capitalism teaches competition, and competition produces winners and losers. In America, guilt is not a necessary or expected by-product. It is one thing to downsize from an SUV to a smaller, more fuel-efficient automobile because the higher cost of gas makes day-to-day usage prohibitively expensive. It is quite another to lay such a guilt trip on a suburban mom about her "carbon footprint" that she chooses to forgo the option to drive her kids around town in a safer, larger vehicle.

It falls to the commonsense majority to understand and articulate the very real difference in attitude brought to bear by this example. Rational decision making may dictate a change in lifestyle because of new or different economic realities. No surprise here. It is the way most responsible individuals run their finances—and lives. Conversely, emotionalism and a mistrust of capitalism foster the notion that upward mobility and consumerism are contrary to the greater good.

We Are the World?

The third aspect of this dangerous approach to economics and culture concerns the role of foreign opinion on the way Americans choose to live their lives.

Then Senator Barack Obama's presidential campaign, particularly his world tour during the summer of 2008, was replete with subtle and not-so-subtle apologies for the way Americans live and consume. No better example presents itself than Obama's comments at a campaign rally in Roseburg, Oregon, in May 2008:

> We can't drive our SUVs and you know, eat as much as we want and keep our homes on, you know, 72 degrees at all times, and whether we're living in the desert or we're living in the tundra, and then just expect every other country is going to say OK. You guys

go ahead and keep on using 25 percent of the world's energy. Even though you only account for 3 percent of the population, and we'll be fine. Don't worry about us. That's not—that's not leadership.[33]

The appetite for such anger at alleged American excess is virtually unlimited—from socialist-inspired slow- or no-growth economies in western Europe to corrupt, third-world autocratic regimes and anti-democratic, despotic rulers of radical Islamic regimes, desperate to lodge additional economic and cultural complaints against a free, wealthy United States. The Barack Obama/Al Gore approach to these foreign audiences is transparent—and effective. The policy goal is American "enlightenment" about our limited resources and the negative impact of the "selfish" U.S. consumer on Mother Earth. This cultural indictment produces guaranteed applause lines in parts of the world resentful of America and its wealth; receptive audiences operating with an anti-American bias are more than willing to buy into the charge that American greed and carelessness drive man-made environmental catastrophes such as global warming. It is not difficult to imagine left-wing journalists from around the world rejoicing at the news: it is all those American imperialists to blame for our substandard economies—their president told me so.

Good and Great America

The fourth and final issue is the foundation of the entire debate. It is what many commentators on the right have labeled "American exceptionalism." Definitions as to what the phrase means abound, but most would concur with the concept of a unique, grand experiment in democracy encompassing God-given individual rights and incredible freedoms, from the ballot box to the marketplace. These freedoms have contributed to the formation of the most powerful economic and military powerhouse the world has ever seen. Magnificent traditions of philanthropic activism, charitable giving, and foreign assistance provide further context to the famous

---

[33] Barack Obama, transcript, "Ballot Bowl 2008," CNN, May 17, 2008, http://transcripts.cnn.com/TRANSCRIPTS/0805/17/bb.01.html.

line attributed to (though never proven to be written by) Alexis de Tocqueville, "America is great because America is good." And, at least for many of us, all of this makes America an exceptional place.

This special status reflects an endless desire to improve all things American. It is a view contrary to the limiting and guilt-edged attitude of the new left. Our cultural enthusiasm for American exceptionalism is a national strength. It gives us confidence. It strengthens our conviction that better days lie ahead. We must protect it and teach it to future generations. Unfortunately, the importance of confidence often seems to be lost on liberals and progressives (and liberals who call themselves "progressives"). They seem to imply that self-doubt is the appropriate grounding for America's future. I am confident they are wrong.

A related point pertains to the positive aspects of rational conservation and science-based environmental protection. Recycling programs, nutrient reduction on farms, rural land preservation, revitalization of older town centers, increased automobile fuel efficiency, upgrades to sewage treatment plants, waste-to-energy technologies, and natural resource management use sound science and technology to improve our quality of life. A further positive outcome from this commonsense approach: reduced dependency on foreign sources of energy. These and other initiatives remain popular because they make sense. None of them, however, require a rejection of American cultural attitudes about upward mobility, wealth creation, the importance of markets, or our hopes for a more prosperous life for us and our children. A worldview that seeks to inculcate a robust, opportunity-laden, confident American economic culture with guilt trips, limited horizons, and egalitarianism *must* be resisted at every turn. Failure to do so will result in the gradual degradation of our standard of living—and the loss of that opportunity society so many have worked so long and so hard to build.

Taking On
the Mortgage Meltdown

*"To the banks and financial institutions: We want investment
in our communities, loans and credit to develop business, and
growth for our communities. We are not going to allow you
to launder drug money and support the pain and devastation
of drugs in our communities while you redline us and deny us
access to credit and investment. Do you hear me, Citicorp?"*

—CONGRESSWOMAN MAXINE WATERS (D-CA),
October 25, 1997. speech at Million Woman March

THE MORTGAGE MELTDOWN OF 2007–2008 hit every American
pocketbook in dramatic fashion. Yet the root cause of the most consequential economic crisis of our time has received minimal in-depth
coverage in the mainstream press. Even on those relatively rare occasions when critical analysis has made its way into the national debate,
more often than not "market capitalism" was offered as the primary

cause of the collapse. "You just can't trust those markets" has been the mainstream media's constant mantra from Day One. Election season 2008 may have been the high-water mark of the anti-market rhetoric as former public interest lawyer and housing advocate Barack Obama, the Democratic congressional leadership, and Democratic candidates around the country sounded the anti-market theme to great effect. An increasingly restless, unhappy American middle class presented a willing audience as the 401(k)-generated wealth of a generation began to disappear—quarterly statement after quarterly statement.

The Obama campaign's populist-inspired criticisms of the mortgage crisis were chronicled on a daily basis by a media all too willing to indict so-called "trickle down economics." Perhaps Obama's strongest criticism was offered in a statement released by his campaign to the press on September 15, 2008, as the stock market continued to tumble and heretofore strong investment banks ran to the federal government for cover—and billions of American taxpayer dollars:

> I certainly don't fault Senator McCain for these problems, but I do fault the economic philosophy he subscribes to. It's a philosophy we've had for the last eight years, one that says we should give more and more to those with the most and hope that prosperity trickles down to everyone else....What we have seen in the last few days is nothing less than the final verdict on an economic philosophy that has completely failed.[34]

For Obama, an aggressive class warfare–based campaign strategy in the middle of a severe economic crisis served its intended purpose by producing a historic win in rather easy fashion. In retrospect, it was the perfect storm: reports of outrageous Wall Street executive compensation, historic declines in the stock market, gasoline near four dollars a gallon, surging unemployment, and a devaluation of the housing market. The combined impact was perfect for a candidate well schooled in the tools of class envy with a charismatic delivery and message of "change." Not surprisingly, the Obama era

---

[34] M. Jay Wells, "Why the Mortgage Crisis Happened," *AmericanThinker.com*, October 26, 2008, www.americanthinker.com/2008/10/what_really_happened_in_the_mo.html.

has produced ever-more-anti-market policies emanating from the executive and legislative branches of the federal government. A familiar lesson here is that serious consequences flow from realigning elections.

The political science lessons of Obama's political strategy are not the focus of this chapter, however. There are plenty of scholarly works devoted to the voter strategies employed in the 2008 campaign. Rather, my focus is on how it is essential that the mortgage meltdown be seen as yet another example of how businesspeople were forced into submission by the forces of political correctness to our economic detriment. As the impact of the mortgage meltdown gradually begins to recede, a commonsense majority must again take heed—heartfelt compassion for the poor and the desire to create an affordable housing legacy do not negate elementary laws of economics. Violations of this premise can and do lead to poor results. In the case of housing policy, they led to an economic crisis of historic proportions.

More than a decade ago, as a freshman Republican congressman assigned to the House Banking and Financial Services Committee, I listened to my Democratic colleagues mince few words about federal housing policy. No law stoked their fire more than the far-reaching Community Reinvestment Act, or CRA, which "encourages" depository institutions to write loans within the communities they serve, particularly low-income communities suffering from a dearth of housing-related investment. During deliberations, much of the debate regarding CRA and its implementation was emotional, befitting the tenor of an issue that impacts class and race in such direct terms. Before we explore how the chickens from that rancorous debate came home to roost, however, a brief history of the CRA is in order.

Community Reinvestment Act

In 1977, then Senator William Proxmire (D-WI) first introduced the Community Reinvestment Act. The stated purpose was to stop the practice of bank "redlining," the act of excluding low-income communities from credit availability.

The impact of CRA on local banks was twofold. One, it increased regulatory oversight to ensure that banks would serve the credit needs of low- and moderate-income communities. Two, it empowered a few community activist groups to further pressure lending institutions to write mortgages in economically depressed areas. Not all community activist groups were created equal, however. A few, such as the notorious Association of Community Organizations for Reform Now (ACORN), were more than willing to demonstrate their hyperaggressive, often outrageous tactics, from the local bank lobby to the halls of Congress. The group's nefarious voter registration activities during the 2008 campaign were part of an extreme agenda first brought to light by Fox News and other conservative media outlets.

Many community-focused groups have played honorable roles within the housing industry; these organizations have sought to educate lower-income individuals as to the basics of homeownership and personal financial planning. Their good work in depressed neighborhoods should never be confused with the "let's get paid" crowd more interested in the Democratic Party's political agenda than providing assistance to poor, unsophisticated homebuyers.

And getting paid is clearly what occurred, as a less-publicized aspect of the law allowed community groups to earn a "finder's fee" for marketing the availability of mortgage loans within lower-income communities. These dollars became additional tools in the activists' playbook; now their manipulation of the CRA would be backed up with real dollars. How real? By 2000, the Senate Banking Committee estimated that up to $9.5 *billion* had been transferred from lending institutions to community groups for services rendered.

By the time I entered Congress in 1995, many lending institutions and most Republican members of Congress viewed the CRA as little more than an expensive regulatory scheme that encouraged questionable lending practices to the detriment of the banks and their alleged beneficiaries—customers with marginal credit. Unfortunately, banks believed they had little choice but to comply, as CRA required bank regulators to review institutional credit practices in low-income neighborhoods prior to approving expansion through additional branches.

The racially tinged rhetoric from my Democratic colleagues on the Banking and Financial Services Committee was ugly and divisive. Even as late as 2008, Rep. Barney Frank (D-MA) and other promi-nent liberals were blaming racism for continued Republican criti-cism of CRA. The sustained focus on race was no surprise, just more of the same from the usual suspects. Yet many of us fully understood why such rhetoric could prove so effective; the economic discrimi-nation inflicted on minority communities over many decades had devastated the upward mobility of generations of African Americans.

So, how should we view a process with such good intentions but so terribly flawed in the hands of irresponsible people? After a steady stream of CRA-inspired debates during the 104th and 105th Congresses, my conclusions were threefold: one, there was likely a legitimate case to be made for the CRA at its inception; two, CRA's reach had grown far beyond its intended boundaries; and three, the end result would bring decidedly mixed results to its intended beneficiaries.

The advent and empowerment of a subprime mortgage market meant that low- and moderate-income individuals with no or mar-ginal credit histories would gain access to home mortgage loans. Some would use their new liquidity to great economic advantage. Others would squander the opportunity, leading to deeper personal financial woes and additional bad debt. Although many observers chose to ignore this inconvenient result, the primary actors—banks, Wall Street investment houses, legislators, regulators, and commu-nity activists—understood the clear trade-off in the policy.

Economic Crisis Replay

There have been plenty of Monday-morning quarterbacks setting forth accurate *and* revisionist retrospectives about the mortgage crisis and resulting economic meltdown. It is a complex story with many players (good, bad, and negligent, but well meaning) thrown into the mix. Accordingly, a familiar and easier-to-understand context is required in order to judge just how easily good intentions can lead to disastrous results. For me, that context is Bob and Nancy Ehrlich, circa 1967, and looking to move from that tiny apartment on Maiden

Choice Lane to that first row house two miles away. But could the Ehrlichs afford to make the big move from renter to owner?

The Ehrlich household included Mom, Dad, and me. The household income was under ten thousand dollars, and the monthly rent was ninety-eight dollars. The godsend of a GI loan provided for no down payment. Dad's sisters would have to pitch in to cover the closing costs. The thirty-year mortgage carried an interest rate of 6 percent. Monthly payments for the $11,200 row house down the hill from the local middle school would be ninety-two dollars a month.

The GI Bill notwithstanding, the Ehrlichs of 1967 fit the financial posture of a "subprime family"—no real credit history, income at the very edge of affordability, no savings to tap, and no financial cushion to fall back on. Yet the first-time homeowners decided to take the plunge, a government-backed mortgage was secured, and a monthly payment was never missed, albeit with not much room to spare. Thirty years later, our Dolores Avenue home has become the most valuable asset the Ehrlichs could have ever hoped to own.

Fast-forward to the new millennium, in which CRA-inspired lending practices stood in sharp contrast to the Bob and Nancy Ehrlich scenario. First, the Clinton administration generated regulations built on the coercive nature of the CRA to further leverage banks into writing additional subprime loans targeted to high credit-risk individuals—often with adjustable rates, little or no down payments, poor or questionable credit histories, and no evidence of the borrowers' income. Then the administration took an enormously problematic next step: it allowed banks to package subprime loans in securities with prime loans. These securities were gobbled up by Wall Street firms and government-sponsored enterprises (GSEs) such as Fannie Mae and Freddie Mac, and then sold to investors around the world. And why not? The products carried the seal of approval from leading Wall Street investment houses. This was a great bargain for all the economic actors involved, including the banks, which were now able to peddle new products, absolve themselves of the considerable risk associated with subprime mortgages, and use the proceeds from the sales to further expand their market in low-quality, high-risk loans.

Another major beneficiary of the subprime pipeline included the major Wall Street investment houses. Their complicity in the great mortgage-induced meltdown has generated another cottage industry of books and movies; unfortunately, most of the story lines encompass tales of greed, negligence, ruined careers, and fire sales of some of our most well-known investment banks. These titans of American capitalism were more than willing to charge huge fees on the packaging and sale of mortgage-backed securities around the world. Boom times ensued and the Wall Street bonus mill exploded—until the smell from all those toxic assets wafted into Americans' living rooms. The resulting demise of some heretofore behemoth investment firms will be analyzed and bemoaned for many years to come.

In retrospect, CRA-inspired mortgage commitments are staggering, beyond the comprehension for most of us not schooled in the ways and means of high finance. In 2009, Peter Schweizer used statistics from the National Community Reinvestment Coalition to quantify CRA-inspired mortgage dollars at risk:

> [I]n the first 20 years of the act, up to 1997, commitments totaled approximately $200 billion. But from 1997 to 2007, commitments exploded to more than $4.2 *trillion*...The burdens on individual banks can be enormous. Washington Mutual, for example, pledged $1 trillion in mortgages to those with credit histories that "fall outside typical credit, income or debt constraints," and was awarded the 2003 CRA Community Impact Award for its Community Access program. Four years later it was taken over by the Office of Thrift Supervision. In 2004 Bank of America agreed to provide $750 billion in CRA loans to applicants with poor credit who had previous difficulty obtaining a mortgage. By 2008 Bank of America was reporting that CRA loans represented only 7% of its portfolio but 29% of its losses. Numerous large banks are now in the middle of enormous CRA commitments. In 2004 JPMorgan Chase agreed to provide $800 billion of such loans over the course of 10 years.[35]

---

[35] Peter Schweizer, "A Poisonous Cocktail," *Forbes*, October 5, 2009.

Perhaps it was the new breed of questionable mortgage lenders that could claim the prize for "Most Greedy." Michael Lewis' chronicles of Wall Street greed are legendary, but perhaps no anecdote better illustrates the bloodlust for dollars than Long Beach Financial, a wholly owned mortgage subsidy of Washington Mutual. According to Lewis, "Long Beach...specialized in asking homeowners with bad credit and no proof of income to put no money down and defer interest payments as long as possible." In one particularly egregious example, an unskilled worker living in Bakersfield, California, with an annual income of $14,000 was lent $720,000![36]

On the GSE front, the new century brought huge debt portfolios and low capital margins. This new era carried with it feel-good themes of universal homeownership and no real regulation of the powerful GSEs that ruled Capitol Hill through fear, intimidation, and an army of highly paid lobbyists. Referencing my House Banking and Financial Services Committee days, I was always impressed by the depth and reach of Fannie's lobbyists—they were plentiful in number and always plugged into the latest committee deliberations. Huge CEO salaries and major accounting scandals constituted mere temporary roadblocks; what could stand in the way of this powerhouse industry? At the time, nothing. It was viewed as integral to the one policy goal glorified by both parties—homeownership.

Periodic Republican attempts to strengthen Fannie and Freddie were met with the by now expected response—how dare you fear-mongering Republicans attempt to limit the dream of homeownership! As usual, the primary Democratic charge was that the government had not gone *far enough* in expanding the subprime market. Witness Barney Frank:

> I do not think we are facing any kind of crisis. That is, in my view, the two government sponsored enterprises we are talking about here, Fannie Mae and Freddie Mac, are not in a crisis...I do not think at this point there is a problem with a threat to the Treasury...I believe that we, as the Federal Government, have

---

[36] Michael Lewis, "The End," Portfolio.com, November 11, 2008, www.portfolio.com/news-markets/national-news/portfolio/2008/11/11/The-End-of-Wall-Streets-Boom/index.html.

probably done too little rather than too much to push them to meet the goals of affordable housing and to set reasonable goals... I think we see entities [Fannie Mae and Freddie Mac] that are fundamentally sound financially and withstand some of the disastrous scenarios.... But the more pressure there is [on these companies], then the less I think we see in terms of affordable housing.[37]

In fact, the government had gone too far, too quickly. By April 2007, *The New York Times* would note that "the democratization of credit" was "turning the dream of homeownership into a nightmare for many borrowers" as 60 percent of the "newfangled mortgage loans" were in foreclosure.[38]

Ironically, in the election of 2008, it was Republicans on the wrong side of public dissatisfaction with the mortgage meltdown and a faltering economy. Even in the aftermath of Fannie and Freddie's receivership, the forced sale of Bear Stearns to JPMorgan Chase, and the failures of Lehman Brothers, AIG, and Washington Mutual, leading Democrats such as Frank and Waters escaped generally unscathed, save for the occasional exposé on Fox News or talk radio. The unrelentingly negative economic news made it impossible for the voting public to distinguish the gross negligence of the congressional Democrats from the greed of the Wall Street firms that packaged and sold mortgage securities from the repeated dire warnings issued by the likes of President George W. Bush, Senator John McCain (R-AZ), Congressman Richard Baker (R-LA), and Federal Reserve Chairman Alan Greenspan. A lone exception to the Democratic state of denial was Congressman Artur Davis of Alabama who, in September of 2008, admitted to what close observers of the mortgage mess had known since the first Clinton administration:

Like a lot of my Democratic colleagues, I was too slow to appreciate the recklessness of Fannie and Freddie. I defended their efforts to encourage affordable homeownership when in retrospect I

[37] House Committee on Financial Services, *The Treasury Department's Views on the Regulation of Government Sponsored Enterprises*, 108th Cong., 1st sess., September 18, 2003.

[38] Gretchen Morgenson, "Home Loans: A Nightmare Grows Darker," *The New York Times*, April 8, 2007.

should have heeded the concerns raised by their regulator in 2004. Frankly, I wish my Democratic colleagues would admit when it comes to Fannie and Freddie, we were wrong.[39]

Good for him. But not so good for the American economy.

Banking in Baltimore

An interesting footnote to this story began in my hometown of Baltimore on January 8, 2008. On that day, the city of Baltimore filed a first-of-its-kind lawsuit in federal district court accusing Wells Fargo Bank of engaging in a "reverse redlining" practice by targeting higher-interest subprime mortgages to black homebuyers in greater frequency than white homebuyers. The suit sought damages from Wells Fargo for making the subprime loans, many of which have since gone into default. In effect, the city of Baltimore filed a civil lawsuit against a major mortgage lender in order to recoup a portion of the costs associated with foreclosed properties located within the city.

My concerns about this litigation do not extend to illegal or inappropriate banking or marketing techniques. For example, to the extent an institution sought to play fast and loose with its advertising, loan documentation, or knowingly had its employees push borrowers toward riskier subprime mortgage arrangements, it most appropriately should face the heavy hand of regulators and the courts. This is as it should be. But such practices are already illegal. Rather, my worries pertain to the millions of honest, hardworking Americans with less-than-stellar credit ratings and the institutions willing to extend them credit. Suppose it is determined at trial that more African American homeowners than white families in Baltimore secured subprime loan products from Wells Fargo, and that those same subprime loans were a function of legitimate credit risk ratings associated with the borrower's personal credit history. What then? CRA encourages riskier loans in poorer neighborhoods in places like Baltimore; isn't it logical, if not predictable, that a lender who

---

[39] James Taranto, "The 'Fact Checking' Fad," *The Wall Street Journal*, October 7, 2008.

seeks to meet its CRA obligations will see a higher number of mortgage defaults when a rapid downturn occurs in the economy? Must lenders curtail making riskier loans in low-income neighborhoods, thereby unraveling the intent of the CRA? Finally, must other institutions now cease extending credit to those most in need in order to minimize their liability? Let's hope not. And let's hope the Baltimore litigation leads to a fair and equitable conclusion for borrowers and lenders alike. People of limited means deserve access to credit, but banks that extend such credit should not be sued for doing what Congress encouraged them to do through regulatory regimes such as the CRA. There are millions of American families, both black and white, whose financial situations are similar to the Ehrlichs of 1967. They should be provided access to credit *when* there is a reasonable expectation they can repay the loan. Now *that's* compassion.

To paraphrase my former colleague Rep. Maxine Waters (D-CA), credit and liquidity are essential for the sustained development of our inner-city communities. To those compassionate advocates who so relentlessly pressured urban financial institutions to extend mortgage credit to families with limited ability to make the monthly payments on those mortgages: you have no standing to blame anyone or anything other than yourselves and your congressional allies. Even good intentions do not a policy make.

Taking Responsibility

That said, additional responsibility must be shared between other major participants: the originators of the riskiest subprime loans, the Wall Street behemoths that packaged and sold the loans, compliant credit agencies, and the fund managers who sought to purchase as many of the subprime-backed loans as possible. Their respective negligent deeds should be viewed in an even more egregious light since they lacked the philosophical zeal that propelled so many advocates within the Democratic congressional leadership and the West Wing during the heady days of the Clinton administration. In other words, at least the members of Congress had their ideologies pushing them forward; not so when it came to the Wall Street purveyors of bad mortgage paper. They had the fast buck in mind, pure and simple.

Many thousands of allegedly bright mortgage professionals built an industry on a house of cards. They engaged in questionable lending and advertising practices on a grand scale. Many gave no thought to the homeownership endgame. But basic laws of economics stood in the way of a government-generated housing utopia, and at the very center of the collapse were the thousands of CRA-generated loans taken out by people who, in too many cases, had little or no ability to make the required monthly payments. To the city of Baltimore and others who wish to make an example of the Wells Fargos of the world—be careful what you wish for as you seek to "protect" citizens with marginal credit. Your last attempt to provide for the less privileged among us helped cause a market crisis that stirred a credit crisis that led to a worldwide recession.

On the political front, the primary miscreants in the crisis did not pay a political price for their actions; most of the major players hailed from safe Democratic seats. Given the dimensions of our subprime mortgage-induced recession, one is left to speculate what type of catastrophe it would take to defeat them at the polls.

Nevertheless, many hearts and minds have been altered as a result of the mortgage finance crisis, not least of which is the recognition, from the most left-leaning administration in recent memory, that government entities and policy played a dominant part in building the catastrophic housing bubble of 2004–2007.

Calls for a new regulatory regime engendered by the credit crisis led to the Dodd-Frank financial overhaul bill passed by the 111th Congress. The law required the Obama administration to submit a GSE reform plan by January 31, 2011. In response, a proposed outline offered by Treasury Secretary Tim Geithner included a *private sector*–oriented finance option—a momentous change of direction given the president's previous activities with the likes of ACORN.

The proposed option followed in pertinent part a recent white paper published by the free market–oriented American Enterprise Institute (AEI). The substance of the proposal called for a newly reinvigorated private mortgage system focused on the issuance of prime mortgages—creditworthy instruments attractive to secondary market buyers. A *Wall Street Journal* piece by AEI Senior Fellow Peter J. Wallison framed the recent history succinctly:

What made the recent financial crisis distinctive was that because of affordable-housing requirements and other policies, half of all mortgages in 2008 were subprime or otherwise risky loans. When the bubble deflated, they began to default in unprecedented numbers. If government policy had not encouraged the origination of these mortgages, we would not have had a financial crisis.[40]

Wallison further notes that 85 percent of potential homebuyers are creditworthy enough to secure prime mortgages, and that the securitization of these investments is always a good bet for investors.

Many commentators have pointed out that even this proposal was not a pure free market alternative, however, as the mortgage-backed securities insured by private firms would enjoy a government guarantee paid for through a fee. The resulting dollars would constitute an emergency fund available to distressed entities running short of reserves.

The approach advocated by the administration and AEI ensures that the intended beneficiaries of the government-inspired "homeownership for all" campaign—the subprime, marginal-credit crowd—will continue to be served through the Federal Housing Administration or another similarly situated entity. Only this time around such (appropriate) assistance will be on-budget and maintained in a way that protects taxpayers. As Fannie's and Freddie's combined losses approach $170 billion, such transparency is indeed a necessary element of federal housing policy going forward.

Republicans and free marketeers of all stripes should welcome one of the few market-driven initiatives advanced by the Obama administration. Indeed, the collapse and resulting fallout of Fannie and Freddie has led all sides of the partisan divide to a common conclusion: a government-subsidized model must be modified in favor of a private-sector approach: private firms, prime loans, market transparency, and appropriate regulation of mortgage underwriting practices. The harsh lessons of giant government-subsidized housing enterprises and forced bad lending practices are now clear for all to

---

[40] Peter J. Wallison, "A Way Forward for the Mortgage Market," *The Wall Street Journal*, February 15, 2011.

see. Privatization is the way forward. It represents a rare opportunity to rein in the reach of the federal government. Indeed, the correct market solution will ensure that policymakers never tread this way again—to the benefit of homeowners and taxpayers alike.

Taking On
the Race Card

"The tendency of the casual mind is to pick out or stumble upon a sample which supports or defies its prejudices, and then to make it the representative of the whole class."

—WALTER LIPPMANN[41]

NOT BACKING DOWN during an attempt to engage in a real discussion of the most volatile social issue of our time—race—is what my idea of political leadership is all about. The problem: instead of adopting that same notion, the left repeatedly uses race as a manipulative tool. Race remains a potent weapon of the left for inducing fear and intimidation in others; it is always available as a divisive yet proven tactic in generating votes from the black community.

---

[41] Walter Lippmann, *Public Opinion* (Minneapolis: Filiguarian Publishing, 2007), 143.

The election of a black president should have diminished the need for such antics, but Barack Obama, the rise of the tea party, and the confusion over the motives of black politicians from the right of the spectrum have only electrified this already explosive issue. My experience in office with race-baiters has taught me that the modern left has a most difficult time accepting people, ideas, and movements that fail to fit into its preconceived stereotypes. It will take much more than a periodic four-year governorship in dark blue states or a few African American congressmen from white districts to chisel away at well-established preconceptions about Republicans in African American communities. The racially charged moments I struggled through strongly reflect what we're seeing right now on the national scene.

Race at the Polls

By September 2002, the battle for the governor's office had begun. Polls showed the race to be a virtual tie. My supporters had an "I-told-you-so" attitude about them. Doubters in Maryland were sitting up and paying attention. Lieutenant Governor Kathleen Kennedy Townsend was worried. The call from her campaign staff came to my office: "Let's debate."

Our side was insistent on format: just one moderator to ignite a "conversation" between the two candidates. This was, by far, my comfort zone. Our negotiator, communications director Paul Schurick, pushed for the minimal rules and a more open-ended discussion format. The Townsend camp would have none of such an open process; it wanted a strictly controlled time limit–enforced "debate," really just a series of point/counterpoint exchanges that would not allow for in-depth analysis. I believe complex issues such as affirmative action, stem cell research, and the budget process required more than simplistic pronouncements. Further, my courtroom training was inconsistent with the easily manipulated sound-bite process I wished to avoid.

As the underdog in the race, however, I needed all the exposure I could muster. I told my staff to negotiate the best terms possible for a live television debate, but in the end I knew I had to take on my well-known, well-financed opponent anytime, anywhere, and in any manner she wanted. Underdog candidates are rarely able to dictate the terms of a prime-time debate.

We agreed to a single debate on the campus of Morgan State University, Maryland's flagship historically black university in Baltimore. In addition to the tens of thousands of Marylanders who would watch the debate on television, fifteen hundred people would attend in person.

If *The Jerry Springer Show* is your kind of entertainment, then you would have loved what unfolded inside Morgan's Murphy Fine Arts Center that night. All along, I feared I would be walking into the political lion's den—and I was right. Even so, I could never have envisioned what went down on that memorable occasion.

An Oreo Debate

Hours before the debate, the grounds outside the Murphy building were crowded with busloads of mostly white union members from Pennsylvania bellowing anti-Ehrlich and anti-Republican rhetoric. Far worse, my staff watched them hand out packs of Oreo cookies in a brutal racial reference to my conservative African American running mate, Michael Steele. Joining the electrified mob of union members were hundreds of young college students who had presumably been whipped up by the Townsend campaign with racially tinged, anti-Ehrlich messages. According to staff, supporters of my campaign were harassed and jeered as they made their way into the building.

By 6:45 P.M., the lower tier of the auditorium was packed. When Michael Steele and his family were escorted to their seats, the jeers began. Students booed. Oreo cookies were tossed. From backstage I heard a loud, sustained boo for no apparent reason. When Greg Massoni, my press secretary, informed me that the invective was directed at my parents, I told him, "It's gonna be a long night."

The fifteen hundred or so people who attended the debate that night witnessed, and in some instances participated in, an ugly spectacle, but the viewers who watched on television at home experienced quite a different event.

Townsend's opening remarks were exactly on script. Her opening remark dug right into a racial nerve. After lambasting me for "opposing affirmative action based on race," she exclaimed, "Well, slavery was based on race! Lynching was based on race! Discrimination was based on race! Jim Crow was based on race!

"Affirmative action should be based on race!" Enthusiastic applause rained down throughout the auditorium.

My opening remarks were met by a chorus of boos and shrieks. I stood at my podium as the boos swept down from the audience. The rancor grew louder. I decided to remain silent until the noise diminished to a tolerable level. Minutes later, the National Association for the Advancement of Colored People's Kweisi Mfume, the host of the debate and a former colleague from Congress, jumped from his seat in the first row of the auditorium, leapt onstage, and pleaded for calm. It was nearly three minutes after my opponent finished speaking before I could utter a word. I thought to myself that at least the worst was over, now things would calm down and we could get to the substance of the discussion. I was wrong.

The debate commenced and Townsend played the race card early and often. Time and again, she challenged me on matters related to race, including a recently released NAACP "report card" that gave a civil rights grade of "F" to most GOP members of Congress, including me.

I responded to questions in a calm tone and with straightforward answers, directing my responses not to the panel of questioners but to Townsend herself. I was itching for a true debate, hoping she would engage me on substantive issues. For the most part, such engagement did not transpire, to my great frustration, a frustration that played out in my overuse of the term "Ma'am" in addressing her. Only later did I realize my cathartic use of this respectful term!

Had the deck been stacked against me? Absolutely, and I knew it the moment I set foot in that huge auditorium: the place was packed with hostile political ringers on the campus of Maryland's leading historically black university; an opponent who played the race card at every turn; and a panel of journalists that, at the last minute, changed to include Lillie Hamer, a "freelance reporter" whom no one on my staff had ever heard of, and who asked the most loaded question of the night. It went like this: "If you [Congressman Ehrlich] will go back for me again and explain, if you will, in more detail [your] failing marks from the NAACP since becoming a member of Congress and also explain, please, your thoughts on [your] failing marks from the National Hispanic Leadership, the Leadership Conference on Civil Rights, and why you voted against hate crime legislation and from banning the use of affirmative action."[42]

It got much worse seconds later when Hamer had the opportunity to ask a question of Townsend. "Yes," Hamer said, "I'd also like you [Lieutenant Governor Townsend] to respond to the same question."

I have a specific recollection of a singular thought running through my mind at the time: *Can this really be happening?* After all the work, conversations back and forth with Kendel, analysis as to whether to leave a safe congressional seat, long hours driving from fund-raiser to fund-raiser, and concern over the myriad details that go into any serious statewide campaign, could it be coming down to such a transparent setup? And, closely following that thought, a mental reminder to ask my press staff how in the world that "freelance reporter" ended up on the panel.

Two hours and one wild "debate" later, I headed out the back door of the auditorium and into a driving rainstorm to discover that our car was covered in Townsend bumper stickers and, we would learn later, a long spike had been driven into one of our tires. In light of what occurred that night, it may be surprising to learn that as I entered the car I turned to Kendel and stated with confidence, "I think we won the election tonight." This was not the majority view in the auditorium, however.

Why was I so confident? Well, I had marched into a political lion's den, taken on biased questions, confronted the questioners when appropriate, challenged Townsend herself, and never once offered the politically correct answer to racially charged questions. From my perspective, so far so good, but there was something more important at work that night. I had taken advantage of the power of live television. Thousands of voters watched live that night, with cameras

---

[42] Lillie Hamer, Morgan State University Gubernatorial Debate, C-SPAN, September 26, 2002, www.c-spanvideo.org/program/172875-1 (accessed August 23, 2011).

trained only on the two candidates, oblivious to the Townsend supporters in the auditorium trying their best to make life difficult for
me, my family, and our supporters. This audience was my real target.

The old adage that candidates must know their audience has become irrelevant. Today, candidates must know their audiences, because there are more than one at all times. At the Morgan debate, my
opponent had the auditorium's audience in the palm of her hand,
but the audience at home—the audience that mattered—saw a shrill,
scripted, race-baiting candidate whose tone did not rise to the level
of an executive. Those same television viewers watched a Republican
candidate who at least spoke to them in a direct, nonthreatening way,
despite too many ma'ams.

Just ask former presidential candidate Howard Dean about the importance of knowing your audiences. His meteoric rise in the 2004
presidential campaign came to a crashing halt due in large part to the
infamous "Dean scream" the night of the Iowa caucuses. While the
shrieking, red-faced candidate may have lit a fire under his audience
in the room that night, he horrified the other audience, the millions
of moderate Democrats watching on television who, until that moment, had actually considered voting for him.

Second, I was willing to bet the race card would not trump substance, at least this time. I held out hope that by 2002 we had progressed further on race than the horrific performance I witnessed
that night. My hope was real, but recent experience at the state and
national level had unfortunately confirmed time and again how use
of the race card could impact elections in ugly, divisive ways.

I had, in fact, lived through one searing, public race-based debate
during my second term in Congress in the Second Congressional
District. Middle-class black flight from persistent social and economic problems in Baltimore had led to the slow but steady assimilation of black families into the rock-solid middle- and working-class
neighborhoods of suburban Baltimore throughout the 1970s and
'80s. I do not pretend this gradual desegregation of metropolitan
neighborhoods was accomplished without a degree of racial tension. Racial hostility has been a fact of Baltimore life for a very long
time. Nevertheless, most of the Beltway communities I grew to
know so well in my youth and as a public official retained their solid

foundations. In the aftermath of the open housing era, the majority of black families who had moved into the suburbs shared a similar socioeconomic status with their new neighbors. This was the classic socioeconomic integration: acceptance, if not always wholesale welcoming, was accomplished because the new arrivals had earned their way into the middle class.

It bears repeating that Baltimore has never been a beacon of racial reconciliation. Desegregation and open housing came grudgingly—and late. It took the civil rights era, open housing initiatives, and an emerging black middle class to achieve a respectable degree of racial integration in suburban Baltimore by the mid-1980s. The fact remains, however, that such integration did occur in many of the towns and communities surrounding Baltimore. Not surprisingly, this dramatic change in racial composition did not enflame racial tensions because similarly situated families tend to share common values. In blunt terms, race becomes less of an explosive element when those economically situated families share approximate income levels and other expectations, such as demand for quality education, safe streets, and efficient transportation.

The converse is also true. Racial and other tensions tend to grow when common worldviews are not shared—where those who have earned their way into a neighborhood are joined by those who have not. Proof of this inconvenient truth may be found in my high-profile fight with the American Civil Liberties Union (ACLU), the city of Baltimore, and the federal Department of Housing and Urban Development (HUD). Such a high-stakes conflict was also one of the more instructive life experiences a young congressman could ever have.

It was subsequent to a partial consent decree, announced in 1996, that my role became more front and center, and confrontational. This partial consent decree, negotiated between HUD, Baltimore Mayor Kurt Schmoke, and attorneys for the ACLU, pertained to three thousand poor, Baltimore-based African American families who were to be given race-based housing vouchers that could be used only in wealthier, mostly white suburban neighborhoods. Predictably, suburban reaction was not good.

As the storm of protests grew and politicians of all stripes headed for cover, I decided to accept an invitation from the Greater Rosedale

Community Council, a leading activist group opposed to the consent decree, to attend and participate in a town meeting–style gathering to be held at a local community college. I accepted and asked for permission to read the most relevant provisions of the decree, with the aid of a large overhead projector set up in the middle of a field house.

On May 17, 1996, well over two thousand vocal constituents showed up for the meeting, where I read aloud and gave critical comment to page after page of the controversial decree, including a question-and-answer session to end the night. Most of the criticism centered on the failure of similar voucher-based housing programs in the recent past. Nonetheless the assembled, although frustrated and angry with the terms of the settlement, maintained themselves well throughout. I knew, however, this type of monumental "in-your-face" event would not be received well by the political establishment. In fact, when the reviews came in, they made me want to scream. A vindictive *Sun* editorial reporter compared me to white supremacist David Duke...David Duke!

Not backing down when your opposition throws the kitchen sink at you is a recurrent theme of this book. Still, I recall wondering in the midst of the consent decree debate whether any public official could participate in a serious conversation on a race-related issue without having to submit to name-calling and general intolerance. Little did I know that my best opportunity to create a real dialogue would arise a mere six years later.

Make the Race Card Go Away

In 2002, Michael Steele's presence on my gubernatorial ticket allowed our campaign to bring the race issue front and center. I consistently dared all Marylanders to "take the race card down." I told every audience, perhaps incorrectly, that the first time the race card failed as an election tactic would be the last time it would be used. Taking issues pertinent to race to a more substantive level of debate was not going to be easy, but I was determined to win on this contentious issue for many reasons, including the seemingly consequence-less trash-talking directed at Steele by the leadership of Maryland's Democratic Party.

Michael Steele's personal story is what our country is all about. He is a self-made scholarship kid, president of the undergraduate student body at The Johns Hopkins University, Georgetown University Law Center graduate, seminarian, corporate attorney, Republican state party chairman, and family man.[43] In public appearances, he is comfortable, telegenic, glib, and well informed. At six foot five and always well dressed, he is an imposing figure in front of any audience, but is especially suited to television. Yet, despite all of his academic and professional accomplishments, he had been repeatedly belittled by leading Maryland Democrats.

On the stump, I drove home my point by asking: What happens to public servants who disparage an African American leader as an "Uncle Tom" and a "token"? In Maryland, they go right to the top. What consequences follow for a black state senator who states that "party trumps race"? In Maryland, she wins reelection. What happens to journalists who editorialize that a successful, articulate African American candidate is worth little "but the color of his skin"? In Maryland, nothing of consequence happens. They continue publishing their ignorance for public consumption.

Some further background is required for those who may find it difficult to believe what you just read.

Rep. Steny Hoyer, the second-ranking House Democrat, told *The Gazette* newspapers in 2002 that "the problem with token candidates like Mr. Steele is that the voters see them for what they are."[44]

Likewise, Mike Miller, the well-respected, long-serving president of the Maryland State Senate, told *The Gazette* newspapers that same year that "[Michael Steele] is the personification of an Uncle Tom."[45]

A year later, the hard-left editorial board of *The Baltimore Sun* endorsed my gubernatorial opponent, Lieutenant Governor Kathleen Kennedy Townsend. The endorsement was no surprise given the paper's shared preference for tax increases and liberal social policies, but the unprovoked insult the op-ed piece hurled at Steele was

---

[43] In 2008 Steele was elected chairman of the Republican National Committee, where he presided over the historic GOP gains of the 2010 midterm elections.

[44] Josh Kurtz, "Ehrlich Taps Steele," *The Maryland Gazette*, July 11, 2002.

[45] La Shawn M. Barber, "The New Black Codes," *Baltimore Chronicle & Sentinel*, November 9, 2002.

nothing short of stunning. On the morning of November 4, 2002, tens of thousands of *Sun* subscribers woke up to read all about the expected praise for Townsend's performance as lieutenant governor and the equally expected condemnation of my performance as a United States congressman. Very few could have expected the choice of words used in comparing and contrasting the two ticket mates:

> One example [of Townsend's improved performance] is her choice of a running mate in retired Adm. Charles R. Larson, a highly principled and deeply respected former head of the Naval Academy whose leadership experience and expertise in management and budget will complement Ms. Townsend's own strengths. By contrast, Mr. Ehrlich's running mate, state GOP chairman Michael S. Steele, brings little to the team but the color of his skin. His choice was a calculated move by Mr. Ehrlich, made all the more crass when it was discovered that Mr. Steele is being paid by the GOP as a "consultant" to run.[46]

The stunning ignorance of this statement may be the single most transparent example of liberal intolerance I have experienced or read about during my fifty-three years on this earth. It did not stop there for Steele, however.

When asked in 2005 if racially tinged attacks against Steele were inappropriate, state senator Lisa Gladden of Baltimore famously told *The Washington Times* that "party trumps race, especially on the national level.... It's democracy, perhaps at its worst, but it is democracy."[47]

In a similar vein, the *Baltimore Jewish Times* in 2002 quoted Townsend openly questioning why "any Jew who really understands the issues could support"[48] my candidacy.

More recently, MSNBC's Chris Matthews reached a new low when he asked Steele if, at GOP convention settings, black delegates were told not to bunch up because a group of blacks sitting together

---

[46] Editorial, "Townsend for Governor," *The Baltimore Sun*, November 3, 2002.

[47] "Party Trumps Race for Steele Foes," *The Washington Times*, November 1, 2005.

[48] "Townsend's Divisive Campaign," *The Washington Times*, October 7, 2002.

("black folks hanging together") would "scare" these (white) people. Mike's answer of, "What are you talking about?"[49] constituted a high-ground response. I'm not so sure I would have maintained my composure in the face of such ludicrous questioning.

Can a Black Republican Be for Real?

Although public humiliation heaped on leading black Republicans by Democratic leadership types is not a new phenomenon, the tone of these indictments was particularly aggressive. It is clear Steele was viewed as a threat even prior to running on our ticket. With respect to the Townsend comment on the Jewish vote, a similar mindset clearly prevails; it is inconceivable for a monopoly mindset to recognize the existence of contrary views or opinion. And, when those contrary views are expressed or given attention in the public realm, they and their advocates must be dismissed at once. Monopolists will not acknowledge black or Jewish support for Republicans because the task would require a level of insight outside their narrow, caricature-driven world.

In light of this unyielding attitude about certain core constituencies and the accompanying mindset members of the group are "supposed" to possess, it was not surprising for Townsend to ignore my strong pro-Israel voting record in Congress and myriad personal relationships within the Jewish community. For her, the simple fact of my party registration meant I possessed a certain values system, a lifetime of evidence to the contrary notwithstanding.

For many, it is impossible to understand why a thoughtful, successful, well-educated African American such as Michael Steele could possibly be a Republican, much less run statewide in blue state Maryland on a GOP ticket. In this context, Steele represented a major threat to the status quo, a threat that had to be belittled before it could gain widespread acceptance. Acceptance would require a rethinking of race and politics; it is not an exercise easily undertaken by those who perpetuate race-based identity politics. It was, however, a priority for me, given my desire to engage the political monopoly on another one of its

---

[49] *Hardball with Chris Matthews*, MSNBC, January 17, 2011.

fundamental principles. I enjoyed pointing out the intolerance of the modern left. It was satisfying, and not very difficult, to punch holes in the small-minded attacks on Steele. It was vital that we did so because for far too long these race-based attacks were viewed as "no-consequence events." In essence, invective was delivered with no negative political repercussions for the offending party.

Rather than engage on the issues, the purveyors of race-based identity politics seek to dismiss any serious threat through a strategy of race-based impeachment. Any outrage from an acquiescent media will be brief, if it exists at all. The damage to a potential threat like Steele will be accomplished; the stereotype will live on. The political monopoly can rest in peace, free of any real threat to its continuance in power. At its core, Gladden's pronouncement that "politics trumps race" means that many Democratic leaders oppose racist tactics against Democrats only. There is a higher purpose when used against Republicans, so all available attack modes are acceptable. Just get the job done is the mantra—and engage your liberal/progressive community as needed.

Does Party Trump Race?

Racial politics in America took on a new twist with the emergence of Barack Obama. In 2008, the senator from Illinois struck a chord with many heretofore uninterested voters, particularly younger voters so often written off by presidential campaigns due to their historical failure to show up at the polls on Election Day.

From a right-of-center perspective, Obama's appeal has been the subject of much discussion and debate. His far-left associations and class warfare rhetoric are, to some extent, overshadowed by the eloquence of his language and apparent transparency of his persona. Skillful in debate, a pleasing smile, and a smart, attractive wife completed a most positive picture. From the primaries through the general election, it was apparent that the Obama appeal reached into some conservative homes—voters to whom Obama's traditional liberalism would have been anathema in a normal year. To this group, Obama's appeal was less about transcending race than a call for change during a time of war

Governor Ehrlich and Lt. Governor Steele on the steps of the Maryland State House.

and economic unease. Nevertheless, a renewed focus on race and race-related, hypersensitive issues has been a cornerstone of the Obama campaign from its inception.

This same Barack Obama, who now desires to lead a national dialogue on race, visited Maryland during the fall of 2006. He came to campaign for then Congressman Ben Cardin, the Democratic nominee for the Senate seat held for twenty-four years by Paul Sarbanes. Cardin's opponent was Lieutenant Governor Michael Steele. Steele had not only thrown a scare into the national Democratic Party through high approval numbers but he was also causing great consternation among national Democrats by polling 20 to 30 percent support among black voters in Maryland. In dark blue states like Maryland, such African American numbers are cause for drastic remedial action by the entrenched Democratic leadership.

So, who better to stem the tide than the hot ticket from Illinois? Who better to remind black Democratic voters that, in this particular circumstance, party needed to trump race?

At historically black Bowie State University, the agent of racial reconciliation assumed a Martin Luther King Jr.–like tone in making his pitch for the white Democrat and against the black Republican.

Obama: "Listen, I think it's great that the Republican Party discovered black people. But here's the thing...You don't vote for somebody because of what they look like. You vote for somebody because of what they stand for."[50]

A few days later, this same U.S. senator visited two black churches in Tennessee on behalf of Harold Ford Jr., my former colleague and five-term congressman who was involved in a tight Senate race with former Chattanooga Mayor Bob Corker. This Barack Obama struck a decidedly different racial tone, however:

"I know that all of you are going to work the next couple of days to make sure it [a Ford victory] happens, because I'm feeling lonely in Washington. I need my dear friend to join me."[51]

---

[50] Larry Elder, "Jimmy Carter and the Elvis factor," RealClearPolitics.com, September 17, 2009, www.realclearpolitics.com/articles/2009/09/17/jimmy_carter_and_the_elvis_factor_98344.html.

[51] Erik Schelzig, "Sen. Obama Stumps for Ford in Tennessee," *The Associated Press*, November 6, 2006.

The appearance of skin tone as a major factor in voter preference was an impossible-to-miss part of the Tennessee message, and a far cry from the issue-based Maryland message. Similarly, it is unfortunate but not surprising that only a Senator Ford but not a Senator Steele could make the country's only black senator feel less "lonely." Here again, party trumps race, to the detriment of party and race in the United States of America.

Unfortunately, this tactic remains effective. There appears to be no serious consequence for following the mindset that all means can and should be used to destroy the inconvenient exception to the "rule." It follows that an inconvenient black Republican must be taken down, or that the Jewish community must be reminded of the pressing need to reject a GOP candidate.

The 'Southern Strategy'

The use of race as a wedge political tactic has been around American politics for a very long time. In the post–World War II era, it may have been Southern segregationist Democrats who opposed civil rights legislation, but it was the Republicans of the late 1960s who perfected a race-based "Southern Strategy" in order to gain the White House in 1968.

There is little doubt white fear and resentment toward the urban race riots of the '60s and race-based social policy such as busing and affirmative action constituted a "Southern strategy" for the Nixon team. On the national level, it achieved spectacular success as formerly blue Southern states have become increasingly red over the past thirty years. What had been the "solid South" for Democrats is now reliable GOP country. Over time, legitimate concerns over emotional social issues, such as race-based college and professional school admissions, reverse discrimination, and an increasingly activist federal judiciary, have softened the raw racial nerve endings of the '60s and '70s. Nevertheless, I subscribe to the view that Nixon-era realignment "success" remains a primary reason for the wholesale failure of the GOP to attract middle-class black votes. The Bush campaign's boast of increasing black support from 9 percent in 2000 to 12 percent in 2004 speaks volumes about the depth of the problem.

Some may point to the 2010 election of two African American Republicans to the House of Representatives as a crack in this tide, but the facts on the ground reflect otherwise; both Congressmen Tim Scott (R-SC) and Allen West (R-FL) are solid conservatives elected in majority white districts. In fact, the elections of Scott and West continue a familiar pattern: African American Republicans elected to the House always emanate from majority white districts. Accordingly, while they represent a racial broadening of the House GOP Conference, their mere election signals no departure from racial-partisan voting patterns established over the last forty years. Only when an African American Republican can secure election with a significant number of minority votes will real progress occur. There is not a great deal of reason for optimism, however. The election of a black president has only increased the racial-partisan divide, with no relief in sight.

Any thoughts on prospects for GOP electoral success in the post–civil rights era must include a deeper understanding about the central role of the church within the African American community.

It is an accepted fact of political life in black communities throughout America that political candidates are expected to attend religious services (and, in many cases, speak to the congregation from the pulpit) during the political campaign season. For most white politicians, it can be an eye-opening experience: services are generally informal and extended, the music is inspirational, and heaping doses of humor are often made a part of the sermon. When two, three, or four offerings are added to the mix, the difference from most mainstream Protestant or Catholic denominations is apparent.

My experiences over twenty years and hundreds of visits to black churches across Maryland were generally positive. I was usually well received by the parishioners, whether worshipping with five thousand congregants in a Washington Beltway megachurch or a few hundred in a Baltimore neighborhood parish. Full bear hugs were often the rule, not the exception. More often than not, I was invited to either the guest microphone or actual pulpit for words of greeting, which were well received, particularly when my message extended to the activities of Kendel, Drew, and Josh. "Family" was and is a cornerstone of this community, and the athletic and academic accomplishments of my children were greeted with the occasional "Amen" or "Hallelujah." "Friendly" and "respectful" are the most accurate terms that come to mind; smiles and sincere greetings are never in short supply. In short, "church" in the black community is an experience, a commitment in time, money, and raw emotion—not a one-hour drive-by prior to the Sunday golf date. The centrality of the church within the community will only grow as additional congregations morph into community social service and entrepreneurial networks, including child care, drug and alcohol treatment, senior housing, and retail.

So, how was a white Republican politician to interpret this experience? In my case, after observing similar reaction to other white Republican candidates over the years, it was about a deep sense of frustration and, at times, disillusionment. Frustration in that I knew enough about voting patterns in African American communities to never confuse cordial receptions with political support; in other words, just because the members welcomed me in such a genuine way did not mean they were going to vote for me. The disillusionment was a product of the frustration in that I now better understood why liberal black and white politicians felt so safe in denigrating the lives and successes of black, conservative Republicans. First, it was easy to do. Second, there would be little or no consequences for even the most disgraceful behavior. Third, it served to perpetuate the near-total hold on black voters enjoyed by Democratic candidates on all levels.

My extensive visits within Maryland's minority communities repeatedly reflected a positive feeling toward the Republican Ehrlich-Steele administration, which included the first black elected statewide official in Maryland's history and an administration that supported many initiatives important to Maryland's African Americans, including record funding for historically black colleges and universities and minority business enterprise reform. Yet, when the same poll respondents were asked which candidate they would vote for governor, the level of support drastically shifted to the Democratic candidate—in fact—*any* Democratic candidate. This pattern of decent approval numbers for job performance but negligible support versus just about any Democrat was not new to me. It was simply more pronounced in our case precisely because policy successes and myriad appearances within black communities had proven relatively successful, though not when it truly counted—on Election Day. The central lesson here is not difficult to discern.

Enter the Tea Party

In 2010, a further challenging element entered the discussion—the emergence of an aggressive tea party movement. Two well-analyzed aspects of the movement pertain to its opposition to the spending practices of the Obama administration and the monstrosity known as Obamacare. The historic federal deficits that followed fueled a surge in a grassroots brand of fiscal conservatism rarely seen in American politics.

I had the opportunity to observe the tea party's grassroots activism from a front-row seat as tea partiers began showing up at rallies, Lincoln Day dinners, and GOP club meetings throughout the 2010 campaign. Some were self-identified Democrats, some disillusioned Republicans, still other libertarians of one stripe or another. All shared at least one common denominator: a disgust with profligate overspending by politicians at all levels and a strong opposition to a federal takeover of health care. On November 3, 2010, this newly styled movement delivered a knockout blow to Speaker Nancy Pelosi's House majority while adding six new GOP Senate seats. A historic net gain of 680 state legislative seats completed a monumental day for Republicans located between the coasts.

Yet another realigning election gave rise to the usual overanalysis from the 24/7-pundit crowd. Nevertheless, it did not take a graduate degree in political science to understand that this was a historic repudiation of the Obama-Reid-Pelosi agenda, particularly with regard to federal overspending and Obamacare. What has been underreported, however, is the impact of the constant Obama-bashing from this newly empowered group—and the repercussions for those of us left in blue, coastal states. For us, this was not a happy day, as Democratic candidates ran strong in Oregon, Washington, California, Massachusetts, New York, and Maryland—yes, particularly Maryland, where my comeback bid got swamped by a large turnout of African American voters in Baltimore and the D.C. sub-urbs. A primary reason was the usual reason—large African American turnout spurred on by a renewed indignation toward conservatives generally, and tea party activists in particular.

I felt tea party backlash early and often during the 2010 campaign. It was particularly pronounced on urban radio, where my periodic appearances were punctuated by angry callers reciting a familiar list of grievances around the "racist" tea party. Sarah Palin was a popular throw-in, in light of her activism and broad support within the movement. Mostly, though, the callers made personal requests of me to repudiate the movement because of its (alleged) inherent racism.

For some observers, the African American anger directed at tea party activists could be traced to the March 20, 2010, Capitol Hill rally held on the eve of the Obamacare vote, where the assembled activists were famously accused of directing racial slurs to members of the Congressional Black Caucus as they made their way through the protesters. The alleged slurs were well reported in the main-stream press, and supported by statements from Congressmen André Carson (D-IN) and John Lewis (D-GA).

The fact that not one video, among thousands actively recording the proceedings, captured proof of the allegations was lost in the emotion of the day.[52] The racial slurs story got reported on all the major media outlets, so it had to be true. Far be it for me to question the motives of Lewis, a former colleague and well-respected hero of the civil rights movement. From my viewpoint, whether he or other Black Caucus members heard a racial insult was almost beside the point—the antagonism between the Black Caucus and the assembled activists had roots far beyond what someone thought he heard (or wanted to hear) in the heat of the moment. Those roots were all about degrading organized opposition to the first black president and his aggressively progressive agenda. This was the first serious political challenge to the Obama presidency, and the emotion with

---

[52] The National Tea Party Federation was so frustrated by the national media coverage that it penned an open letter to Chairwoman Barbara Lee of the Congressional Black Caucus requesting any and all "video, audio, interviews, first-hand accounts, etc." of any supporting evidence for the use of racial epithets during or subsequent to the March 20 rally at the Capitol. No response was received.

which it was delivered was guaranteed to light up a Black Caucus now fully informed as to how this movement could block, stop, and injure that president.

A complete investment in the Obama administration required that any real opposition had to be demonized—the sooner, the better. My experiences on black talk radio and in public forums were just shrapnel from this main event. But it had one serious consequence for me and others similarly situated—a "statement" turnout on Election Day. The investment in Barack Obama had to be protected.

The foregoing leads to one of two options for GOP candidates: either give up on black votes at this point in our political history or continue to push against a heavy wall of historically induced racial distrust. I chose to fight, albeit with the knowledge that the daunting task is a bit easier when holding public office, as opposed to throwing stones from the bleachers.

Again, a sense of historical perspective is needed here as well; it was not so long ago that the party of Abraham Lincoln was matched against segregationist Democrats from the South and West at the very beginning of the civil rights movement. The aforementioned "Southern strategy" of the 1960s subsequently began the steady decline of black support for the GOP, which, by the beginning of the new millennium, had reached an embarrassing all-time low. Despite Election Day evidence to the contrary, any serious attempt to resuscitate the GOP must begin with the churches. It is at this central institution where people are most apt to accept a message of individual empowerment, protection of traditional marriage,[53] entrepreneurism, and family values—positions associated with GOP candidates today.

---

[53] Traditional marriage remains a cornerstone position within the black church but with quite limited political consequences for noncompliance. To wit, my 2010 unsuccessful campaign for governor attracted the strong support of black clergy, particularly in majority African American Prince George's County, Maryland. My endorsement from a large coalition of said clergy (complete with printed pamphlets distributed on Election Day) was based in large part on my steadfast support for traditional marriage. Never had so many African American pastors been so out front in support of a Republican candidate. Alas, when Election Day rolled around, the Democrats carried the day by an astounding margin of 92 to 8 percent among black voters.

Don't Let Race Tactics Divide Us

Many books have been written about race and politics in America. It remains a fascinating subject for political and social commentary. My purpose in reviewing the Morgan debate, the Democratic leadership's misuse of race, and the central role of African American churches is to convey an important admonition for any individual or candidate facing a race-based attack from the left. The advice is as follows:

Take it down. Take it down completely. Take it down at every opportunity. Never back off. Make it uncomfortable if you must, but never indulge anyone or anything that seeks to divide by race. Anything less leads to a perpetuation of racial stereotypes completely at odds with our goal of an honest, caricature-free dialogue on race.

Taking On
Failing Education

"Poverty has many roots, but the top root is ignorance."

—Lyndon Baines Johnson

IT'S A FACT OF LIFE for elected officials to visit schools. We see them all—public, private, religious, rural, suburban, and urban. We sit in the tiny chairs at Head Start programs, walk the halls of elementary, middle, and high schools, and talk a little and listen a lot at colleges and universities. These visits are a constant on a public official's calendar, and during my stints in the state legislature and Congress, and as governor of Maryland, mine was full of them.

After I became a parent, I paid even closer attention on these visits and grew to appreciate the special talents needed to be an effective teacher or principal. My typical approach during visits with high school and college kids is to engage on issues *they* wish to discuss. If

I am going to invest a couple of hours in a school visit, I want it to be worth everybody's time—including mine.

We always had plenty to talk about—the political climate in Congress, stem cell research, gun control, terror, civil liberties, Title IX, censorship, the role of the press, and the private lives of politicians. We never failed to have a lively conversation, perhaps most memorably on the impeachment of President Clinton. It was an emotional issue on which everyone had an opinion and everyone wanted to be heard.

My visits to elementary and middle schools in poor and working-class neighborhoods were equally memorable. These children also wanted to be heard; they had dreams and hopes for the future they could express, with a vividness and certainty that was powerful. Whenever I asked, "What do you want to be when you grow up?" answers were what you might expect—"doctor," "teacher," "ballplayer," "artist," and "president of the United States"—regardless of the socioeconomic background of the students. It was clear that at this tender age, there was no difference between the poorest and wealthiest children when it came to how they imagined their futures.

This was not only deeply heartening to me but also disturbing, because invariably this positive vision of the lives and careers they might have would change so dramatically once these students reached their late middle school and high school years. It was as if a lethal one-two-three punch of puberty, a substandard education, and the reality of their neighborhood environment hit them at once, and suddenly the hopes and aspirations that had lit up their young faces were gone.

To see their joy turn to indifference, and their tenderness to hardness, was as harsh a truth as I have had to face in public life. These aren't kids who would be fighting to out-ace each other in Advanced Placement exams or to win National Merit scholarships. For the most part, these were lives that were finished before they started. And the question that haunts me more than ever is, "How do we break this familiar narrative?" How do we change the dynamic that causes us to "lose" so many kids at such an early age? There were two particular school visits that provided me with critical insight and understanding into these difficult questions. These "field trips" did more to shape my perspective on public schools, race, and socioeconomic factors than any academic study or political debate could ever do. And the light went on about what needs to be done to maintain that wonderful optimism I observed in so many second graders.

First Field Trip to the Inner City and a Reading Challenge

The first of these visits occurred in 2001, during my fourth and final term in Congress. I was touring an inner-Baltimore elementary school as part of a campaign to encourage literacy and, of course, to discuss my love of reading. School officials ushered me into a classroom of African American kids who greeted me with cheery enthusiasm. The questions were of the usual variety—how many limos did I have (none); how many "Secret Service agents" followed me around (none); what was President Bush like (very cool); and what was the name of my son (Drew) and where did he go to school (Naval Academy Primary School).

On this particular day, I proposed a challenge to these students, and as a result, I learned as much about the instructor as I did about the class. I dared this class of approximately thirty kids to read a total of sixty books in their free time before the school year ended, and if they succeeded, I would invite them to my Capitol Hill office for a pizza celebration. The kids were clearly thrilled with the challenge and the prospect of spending a day in the nation's capital (or anywhere!) eating pizza.

Just before I left, the teacher pulled me aside not to thank me but to scold me.

"Please, Congressman, why would you challenge these kids like that when we both know they're never going to read those books?"

At first I was surprised by this admonition. Then I was angry. I realized in this moment that I was now a firsthand witness to the "soft bigotry of low expectations"—a phrase President Bush had notably used during the 2000 presidential election. In this teacher's mind, the class of mostly poor black kids would fail to meet my reading challenge since it was not an expectation set for them in their classroom and, most likely, in other aspects of their lives. I wondered what other academic or life challenges and opportunities were not being presented to them because of their class, skin color, or absent parents and mentors. In my mind, this experience became Example A in how *not* to reach children in difficult circumstances. Kids in more difficult environments *need* to be challenged far more than children from wealthier families and high-quality school districts. For most, the absence of challenge amounted to a life sentence of marginal academic achievement, underemployment, or worse.

I left that classroom with a seething kind of despair—so much so that I repeated the incident to my staff and during public forums for many years thereafter. The only balm for my anger came months later when, to my great joy, I was informed the class had met my reading challenge. I had never been so happy to throw a pizza party in my career.

Second Field Trip to the Inner City, and Police Supervision

The second memorable experience took place in October of 2004. I was scheduled to visit Lake Clifton High School in a crime-ridden neighborhood of East Baltimore, a challenging environment under any circumstance, made more so by yet another tragedy. The day prior to my visit, sixteen-year-old Ray Savoy was gunned down near his mother's home in a public housing neighborhood. Savoy's murder was the thirty-first homicide of a person under eighteen in Baltimore that year. My Maryland State Police detail was far more uptight than usual, to the point where cancellation of my appearance had been considered.

Baltimore police had a heavy presence on the Lake Clifton campus when I arrived the next day to speak to a group of high schoolers. As expected, our discussion focused on the previous day's homicide. One after another, the students poured their hearts out about the killings, drugs, guns, and lives of their friends who had dropped out of school. One young football player crystallized the fine line these kids walk every day.

"He was from the projects," senior Michael Nicholson said of Savoy. "Whenever you come from a bad environment and you try to do something good, everyone tries to stop you."[54]

---

[54] Ryan Davis, "Killing Teen Provokes Questions about Violence," *The Baltimore Sun*, October 29, 2004.

"So," I asked, "how do you resist the folks in your neighborhood who want you to deal drugs or commit crimes?" This was not a rhetorical question. These students lived and breathed this dangerous situation on a daily basis.

"I've already seen the other side," Michael said. "I'm trying to see a different side."

"What turned you around?" I asked.

"My brother got killed."

"If your brother had not been killed, would you still be out there?"

Michael nodded. Despite the negative surroundings—the troubled school, drugs, persistent violence, and declining neighborhoods—I could see these students had incredible resiliency. Unlike so many instances in which young teenagers lost their enthusiasm to succeed due to their environment and family circumstances, these kids were determined to perform well in school, determined to graduate, determined to go to college, and determined to meet their career goals. This day, they were determined to, in the words of a female student, make people "in the suburbs" believe that not all kids at Lake Clifton got into trouble. She did not want television to further stereotype her school in such a negative way. She asked if I would take her plea to other schools and audiences over the course of my tenure. I did, over many subsequent months, especially to the white suburban audiences she was so concerned about.

I, too, was concerned about how Maryland's more comfortable citizens viewed the dysfunction in the city schools; these suburbanites *had* to care if we would ever generate a critical mass behind a call for fundamental change in the city school system.

Put Kids First in Education

These two stories are the best illustration of my mindset about the importance of education for every child, but especially those who have been dealt a difficult hand in life, and who are most in need of quality public school education. And why it is so vital for every stakeholder—Republicans and Democrats, voters, parents, and students—to continually challenge the teachers' unions and others in the education establishment to put kids first—even if it means competition from public charter schools, or a merit-pay program based on performance over seniority, or the turning over of a failing public school to a private vendor. The conservative value of healthy competition *can* operate to solve seemingly intractable problems.

The Baltimore City Public Schools had been dysfunctional for many years. Its fiscal problems had garnered headlines all over the country. In the words of the 2006 "Annual Report on Current Progress of Baltimore City Schools," a performance audit found "pervasive lack of controls and included inadequate monitoring of contracts and vendor payments; insufficient or missing documentation; lack of formal processes and procedures in some areas; and failure to follow procedures where they do exist." These and numerous other systemic failures had led to periodic budget deficits and exceedingly high dropout rates that have remained a persistent source of frustration for those intent on righting the ship.

Despite this record of dysfunction and failure, Baltimore's elected officials and most of its delegation in the Maryland General Assembly have repeatedly fought off attempts to impose accountability measures in return for additional state dollars. By 1997, however, with fully one-third of Baltimore public schools qualifying for remedial restructuring, it was clear to all that some degree of autonomy would be lost if the city wished to secure an additional $254 million in state money over the next five years. The result was an agreement in which the governor of Maryland and Baltimore's mayor would make joint appointments to the city's Board of Education. In exchange, the city would receive a quarter billion dollars of new money. City leaders, including the highly respected NAACP chairman Kweisi Mfume, criticized the legislation as an insult to a majority African American Baltimore. In a letter delivered to members of the legislature, Mfume, former Congressman Perrin J. Mitchell, and a number of leading black pastors used strong language to oppose the deal. Their statement read: "We will not accept Baltimore becoming a colony of the State, with its citizens having no say in the education of their children. [The bills enacted] are anti-democratic and smack of racial paternalism."[55]

---

[55] Thomas W. Waldron and William F. Zorzi Jr., "Blacks Denounce Schools Package Management Reforms, Aid Labeled an Affront to Baltimore Residents," *The Baltimore Sun*, April 4, 1997.

The legislation nevertheless passed, as some city and a majority of suburban legislators voted to impose what they claimed would be a degree of accountability in exchange for additional dollars from state taxpayers. Unfortunately, the new governing agreement lacked any real element of oversight; operational control of the city schools was never placed in the hands of the superintendent or state board. The sole partnering arrangement remained the joint-appointment power. Additional dollars and oversight from the state did not constitute a transfer of control.

It will come as no surprise that this limited "city-state partnership" failed to achieve measurable progress over the succeeding years, despite a constant stream of new dollars funneled into the city school budget from the state and federal governments. Despite all good intentions, the additional dollars and joint-appointment process failed to deliver much of anything new, other than an inferior education to many thousands of kids at an exceptionally high price for the taxpayers.

The experience of negligent management and consistent educational failure is not unique to Baltimore. Many urban school systems serve a disproportionate number of poor children who, in many cases, lack desperately needed parental involvement. Despite the infusion of billions of state and federal dollars over the past thirty years, there has been precious little progress to report. Baltimore's experience over this same time frame reinforces the notion that additional dollars do neither a school system nor a supportive, functional family make. Countless books and academic studies have analyzed these perpetually failing systems and their problems. Many more have called for radical policy responses—from tuition tax credits and vouchers to public charter schools and the wholesale privatization of failing systems.

In 2003, the Ehrlich administration pushed through the first charter school law in Maryland history. We did so over the fierce opposition of the state teachers' union and others opposed to competition within the public school system. This policy "win" against long odds and entrenched opposition was a cause for celebration, made more pronounced as dozens of new charters popped up around the state over the next three years. Now there was new hope for kids in the

worst of the worst neighborhoods and stuck in the worst schools—
new hope that we could keep those children on a positive career path
despite their often dire family circumstances.

A Disaster from the Get-Go

All of which leads to the most disillusioning event I encountered in
my twenty years of public service. The issue involved the Maryland
State Board of Education's attempt to impose remedial measures
on the city's worst-performing middle and high schools during the
spring of 2006. That year, the system appeared more troubled than
ever after rejecting four different city schools CEOs over just four
years. Two years prior, with the system facing a crippling $58 million
deficit, and with renewed allegations of fiscal mismanagement, I had
responded to the city's request for additional money with my own
counteroffer: the requested money would be supplied contingent
upon authority to implement appropriate accountability measures
to secure the results Baltimore's children and Maryland's taxpayers
deserved.

A familiar story line led to a familiar response as city leaders and
their allies in the teachers' union rejected my offer out of two very
different concerns: either the traditional fear that a state bailout
would bring additional loss of local control over its schools, or a
partisan fear born out of a deep suspicion about a Republican's ability to follow through on promises made to an African American city
and hostile legislative delegation. Tragically, the city continued to
wallow in a lack of educational leadership, a meddling city hall, and
horrible school performance numbers. Now, however, with newly
revealed, spectacularly dysfunctional test scores dominating the
headlines, we would do very public battle with Baltimore's powerful
educational establishment. This time with strong public sentiment
on our side . . . or so we thought.

For most of my time as governor, it seemed that just about every
week brought stunningly negative revelations about the Baltimore
public schools. With each passing day, I continued to lose confidence
in the management of the school system. By 2006, the facts reflected
systemic failure.

- Of the 189 public schools in Baltimore, eighty-nine (47 percent) were in some stage of "School Improvement"; fifty-four (29 percent) were in the deepest stage of "School Improvement Restructuring Implementation."[56]
- Six schools were identified as being "Persistently Dangerous" as required by federal law. No other school system in Maryland had even one school identified as Persistently Dangerous.[57]
- At all levels (elementary, middle, and high) Baltimore had the lowest attendance rate of all twenty-four school systems.[58]
- According to a report by *Education Week,* of the fifty largest school systems in the United States, the city of Baltimore was ranked number forty-nine with a graduation rate of 38.5 percent. Neighboring Baltimore County was ranked number three with a graduation rate of 81.9 percent. That's a stunning difference of 43.4 percentage points.[59]
- Baltimore's dropout rate remained three times the state average.[60]
- Baltimore had the notorious distinction of the highest percentage of teachers who had not completed the education courses and/or student teaching required for certification out of all school systems in Maryland.[61]
- In Baltimore, only 35 percent of kindergarten students were rated as "fully ready" to enter school, despite robust Head Start and prekindergarten programs in place for years.
- The performance of Baltimore's students on the High School Assessment Tests in Algebra, English 2, and Biology remained the lowest among the state's twenty-four school systems.[62]
- The Maryland State Prosecutor achieved ten convictions in corruption cases pertaining to Baltimore City public schools.

---

[56] 2006 MD Report Card, Maryland State Department of Education.
[57] Gadi Dechter and Liz Bowie, "A Look at Ehrlich's School Criticism Analysis," *The Baltimore Sun,* August 19, 2006.
[58] Ibid.
[59] Ibid.
[60] Ibid.
[61] Ibid.
[62] Ibid.

In the ten years since the passage of the city-state partnership, Baltimore had consistently been given more time to improve achievement in its troubled schools. Little or no progress was forthcoming, despite the fact that Baltimore was now receiving more funding than any other jurisdiction—$9,446 per pupil in 2006. By comparison, the statewide average was $5,362 per pupil.[63]

The facts surrounding this latest saga were not difficult to understand. In March 2006, the predominantly Democratic membership of the Maryland State Board of Education, appointed by my predecessor and me, voted to intervene in the eleven lowest-performing schools in the city, making Maryland the first state in the nation to invoke the remedial terms of the federal "No Child Left Behind" law.

Upon receiving the news, I was pleased for the opportunity to do something extraordinary for kids stuck in the worst educational environment possible. I realized this was a rare chance to try to make a real difference in the lives of young people stuck in difficult circumstances. In the public realm, I saw it as a unique opportunity to generate a new coalition willing and able to take on an education establishment consistently supportive of the status quo despite consistently dismal results over so many years.

The Clash of Politics and Education

After twenty years in public office, it takes a lot to surprise me. But what occurred next stunned me and shocked my conscience. It remains the worst and most indefensible example of raw politics trumping the interests of kids I have ever observed.

Within days of the Maryland State School Board's action, the leaders of the General Assembly rammed through a bill prohibiting the State Superintendent of Schools, Dr. Nancy Grasmick, a national education expert and longest-serving appointed superintendent in the nation, and the state school board from intervening in the city schools. I lobbied fiercely to kill the bill, and I lobbied even harder after I vetoed it to prevent the legislature from overriding my veto. My veto message was quite direct, and read as follows:

---

[63] Ibid.

In accordance with Article II, Section 17 of the Maryland Constitution, today I have vetoed House Bill 1215—*Baltimore City Public School System...*

In its current form, House Bill 1215, which may violate the Constitution of Maryland and other laws, would prohibit the State Board of Education and the State Superintendent of Schools from implementing badly needed restructuring efforts in Baltimore City public schools until May 30, 2007. The major restructuring efforts referenced in the bill include changes to a school's governance, such as removing a school from the control of the Baltimore City Board of School Commissioners. Specifically, the bill blocks or delays the actions taken last month by the State Board of Education to improve Baltimore City schools. Implementation of this bill will circumvent the authority of the Maryland State Board of Education, lock children into a failed system, and may jeopardize $171 million in federal funding for all of Maryland's local school systems... The Maryland State Board of Education identified the 11 schools as low performing in 1997 or earlier. When the schools were identified, the Baltimore City Public School System was informed that under the State's educational accountability system the identified schools were subject to State intervention, including removing the schools from City oversight, if achievement did not improve. Maryland's educational accountability system—which is still in place but jeopardized by this bill—was initiated by Governor Schaefer's Commission on School Performance and predates the federal *No Child Left Behind Act* by a decade.

Baltimore City has had several years to improve achievement in these 11 schools, but little or no progress has been made despite the fact that Baltimore City receives more State funding per pupil than any other jurisdiction. In the four high schools identified for alternative governance, achievement and graduation prospects for students are dismal. Since 1994 an estimated 10,000 students have dropped out of these four schools. On the average, students are absent 36 days, or over seven weeks, per year. An overwhelming majority of students have failed the High School Assessments. In Southwestern's freshman class of 2005, an estimated 99 students out of 100 will not pass the High School Assessments because they cannot read or because they do not understand math. At Frederick Douglass, only 1.4 percent of students passed the High School Assessment in biology and only 4.8 percent passed the High School Assessment in algebra. Clearly, the data present a call to action that the State of Maryland cannot ignore.

Further, we all should be deeply troubled that House Bill 1215 will prevent the State from executing its responsibilities under the federal *No Child Left Behind Act* and State school accountability regulations. An inability to intervene in low-performing schools with "a major restructuring of a governance arrangement" strikes at the heart of accountability. According to the U.S. Department of Education, if this bill becomes law, $171 million in federal Title I funding for all jurisdictions in Maryland may be jeopardized, and the net effect could be a loss of learning opportunities for children in Baltimore City and across Maryland. I cannot permit that to happen.

I reference the enduring words of the 1989 Governor's Commission on School Performance:

All children can learn.

All children have the right to attend schools in which they can progress and learn.

All children shall have a real opportunity to learn equally rigorous content.

For children in the 11 schools identified for alternative governance, these are broken promises.

Baltimore City has had ample opportunity to improve these schools. The children have the potential to learn, indeed to prosper. The dire academic situation demands quick action and any delay will accomplish nothing. The Maryland State Board of Education's actions were not precipitous; they were based on years of solid data and provide us with a carefully drawn blueprint for building a future for thousands of children too long ignored.

How many more generations of future nurses, teachers, elected officials, and successful citizens will live lives of unrealized dreams and should we condemn to despair by our failure to act? I urge the Maryland General Assembly to allow the Maryland State Department of Education to do its job on behalf of our children.[64]

I believed this would be one of those rare cases where the sheer dysfunction of an infamous school system would weigh so heavily on the legislature's collective conscience that even some of the most liberal members would agree to a fix—one that allowed the state to convert the most-distressed schools into public charter schools or to transfer authority to an independent, third-party vendor. Who in the world could argue that *this* degree of dysfunction could be acceptable in twenty-first-century America? The numbers:

Southwestern High School:
- 8.9 percent of students read proficiently.
- 1.6 percent of students are proficient at math.
- For Southwestern's freshman class of 2005, ninety-nine out of one hundred students will not pass their High School Assessment tests because they cannot read or perform math concepts.

Frederick Douglass High School:
- 15.8 percent of students read proficiently.
- 3.5 percent of students are proficient at math.
- 1.4 percent of students passed the biology component of their 2005 High School Assessment.

Patterson High School:
- 18.5 percent of students read proficiently.
- 9.9 percent of students are proficient at math.
- 15.9 percent passed the English component of their 2005 High School Assessment.

---

[64] Robert Ehrlich, veto message on HB 1215, 2006 Laws of Maryland, Chapter 59, April 7, 2006, http://mlis.state.md.us/2006rs/veto_letters/hb1215.pdf (accessed August 23, 2011).

Northwestern High School:

- 21 percent of students read proficiently.
- 6.6 percent of students are proficient at math.
- 8.8 percent passed the government component of their 2005 High School Assessment.[65]

Even the political environment seemed to be working in our favor. A looming election could only help as incumbent legislators could now point to new accountability measures in Maryland's most troubled school system as proof of their commitment to quality education and their determination to ensure at least some degree of accountability for those ever-increasing tax dollars flowing to Baltimore.

In the annals of "just plain wrong," my prediction would prove to be world-class. My personal meetings with legislators produced nothing but statements from members that this vote was "a leadership call," or "a union call," or that they "must ensure the Republican governor does not dictate to our Democratic Party" call. I remember two conversations in particular. Names are not supplied to protect the unconscionably guilty, but both conversations took place in my office on the eve of the General Assembly's veto override vote.

The first was with a Washington, D.C.–area African American legislator who had become a sometime-ally over the years, particularly when educational opportunity was at issue. Her periodic high-profile fights with the leadership reflected an independent streak I admired. Her demonstrated interest in education and educational reform only added to my sense of optimism.

Upon entering my office, this legislator began to brag about her grandson flourishing at an elite private school in Washington, D.C., where tuition costs ran into the tens of thousands of dollars. I told her how happy I was for her grandson, but that our conversation was about kids who had to worry about where their next meal was coming from, about kids who had to share textbooks with classmates during lessons, about kids who were being pushed through a system

---

[65] David Keelan, "O'Malley and Education," *Howard County Maryland Blog*, March 30, 2006, http://hocomd.wordpress.com/2006/03/30/omalley-and-education/.

on a social promotion basis, about kids who had far better odds of serving time in juvenile or adult detention centers then attending the University of Maryland.

Her response? "Sorry, Governor, you will have to work this out with the president of the Senate." In effect, this was an issue that was too hot and too full of political consequences for her to get involved. The fact that the senator had already announced her intent to retire did not seem to be a factor in her decision. The union establishment must be protected at every turn.

Another striking conversation took place with a veteran senator who raised concern over organized labor's aggressive reaction to our initiative. The pragmatic side of the senator's concerns was understandable, in that the private sector unions had come to the aid of the city teachers' union in a public way. In a union-dominated state such as Maryland, this was a powerful coalition. It was the union hypocrisy that struck me at that moment, however. How else could one view a stance that aimed to keep poor kids in failing schools as a convenience to a powerful teachers' union? A once-proud union movement built on the value of hard work, educational opportunity, and economic security was now acting to deny a better life for thousands of kids in terrible situations—and not enough people in positions of authority appeared willing to do anything about it!

Union power made the ultimate outcome a foregone conclusion. My lobbying sessions were spectacularly unsuccessful. My veto was overridden, after which a group of Baltimore Democratic members and jubilant union activists held a "victory" rally, at which they promised to do better in the future, gave heartfelt "thank-yous" to the politicians who defended them, and celebrated a major political defeat for the State Board of Education and my administration. And not very much was said about so many schools failing so many kids, leading to so many broken lives. It was the triumph of politics over people—a "triumph" we will pay for in lost opportunities and wasted lives—an inconvenient truth that must not be lost as union politics and a clear racial divide continue to constitute major obstacles to fundamental educational reform within our urban school districts.

More Pushing by the Unions

The power of big-city public education unions has been investigated by scholars for decades. One of the most thorough analyses on the subject is a 1997 article by Sol Stern published in the *City Journal*.[66]

Stern's analysis examined two basic empirical facts of urban education: one, the absence of a consistent relationship between rapidly growing school budgets and improved student performance, and two, the tendency of restrictive classroom work rules to undermine the teacher-student relationship.

The raw political power exhibited by the Baltimore teachers' union in the spring of 2006 reflects the nationwide trend of ever-expanding union political strength in the face of dismal academic results from the vast majority of big-city school systems. In Stern's view, this relationship is easily explained:

[T]he $250 billion public education industry behaves precisely like any other publicly protected monopoly. Union negotiators in the *private* sector know that if they insist on protecting incompetent workers and cling to outdated work rules, especially in the global economy of the nineties, the company will begin losing market share, and union members will lose their jobs. In public education, by contrast, collective bargaining takes place without the constraining discipline of the market. When school board representatives sit down with union officials to negotiate a labor contract, neither party is under pressure to pay attention to worker productivity or the system's overall competitiveness....After all, most of the monopoly's customers, the schoolchildren, have nowhere else to go. Historically, tax revenues have continued to flow into the schools no matter how poorly they perform.[67]

The mostly poor kids stuck in Baltimore's "worst eleven" indeed had "nowhere else to go" after the General Assembly's infamous vote that spring day. For me, the disappointment was profound and

---

[66] Sol Stern, "How Teachers' Unions Handcuff Schools," *City Journal*, Spring 1997.
[67] Ibid.

permanent. I knew the issue would not be revisited in the near future. The obvious dysfunction was an embarrassment, even if no remedial actions were to be taken.

I was unable to put the aforementioned postvote celebration out of my mind, however. The celebrants knew the cold, hard realities of those schools—that African American males who drop out of high school face a 72 percent unemployment rate in their twenties, and a 60 percent chance of incarceration by their midthirties. All involved were aware that the four public high schools at issue had suffered ten thousand dropouts since 1994. Yet a coalition of the willing was outgunned by a coalition of the status quo; and another attempt at reform was put to rest. As a Republican who has attempted to maintain a healthy respect for notions of federalism, state intervention in local school governance does not come naturally. The mantra of local control supervised by local school boards and local PTAs is not just familiar; it is the appropriate model for public education in our country. Yet I could not accept the habitual failure of the largest school system in Maryland. To do so would have required a repudiation of what I knew the law to be—that each child had a vested constitutional right in securing a quality education, regardless of family income.

The message I conveyed was the same everywhere I went—you *must* care about these kids on three crucial levels—moral, constitutional, and pragmatic. "Moral" because these children are human beings, no different from my own; "constitutional" because these kids were being denied their legal right to an adequate public education; and "pragmatic" (when the first two approaches failed) because these were the future problem adults if we failed to provide educational opportunities leading to a better life. Just about everyone understood the message of "fix the system now"—or pay enormous social costs at some point in the future.

The teachers' union/Democratic establishment reaction was even more telling, if not predictable. My initial low expectations were more than met, as a "circle the wagons," siege mentality took hold from the moment the proposed plan broke. My public pleas for support were fairly reported by the media, but had no measurable impact on the conscience or voting behavior of those suburban Democrats in whom I had invested so much hope. In fact, those so-called moderate Democrats who I just knew would be sensitive to calls for accountability from their more conservative constituents were unresponsive, a shock for me in an election year in which just about every poll reflected "Education" as the number-one issue with voters at the state level.

Election Day 2006 did not provide the "day of reckoning" I had hoped for harking back to that pivotal override vote. In fact, the entire ugly episode had no apparent impact on the voters; the national anti-war vote swept suburban, left-leaning Democrats back into office. If anything, this chapter reflected a coarsening of attitudes toward any attempt at educational reform not endorsed by a teachers' union, a daunting reminder for those wishing to effectuate substantive reform within some of our most troubled public school systems.

Two years after the veto override, there was a sense of (almost) "all quiet on the Baltimore City schools front." Sure, the status quo politicians and appointed officials survived a scare in the spring of 2006. And, not surprising, the spring of 2008 saw a dramatic increase in assaults against teachers in many of these same "persistently dangerous" and failing schools. (In retrospect, how interesting is the union claim that violent incidents are underreported by school administrators for fear of the "persistently dangerous" tag under "No Child Left Behind"!)

The sad fact remains, however, that precious few politicians in either party are willing to take up the plight of the thousands of kids stuck in the Baltimore City Public Schools. So now what?

School Vouchers

Consider the educational voucher controversy that took place in neighboring Washington, D.C., after the 2008 presidential election. The high-stakes political fight that erupted in the U.S. Senate concerned the wildly popular D.C. Opportunity Scholarship Program that generates vouchers for approximately two thousand low-income children in order for them to attend expensive religious or private schools. Note that the program's entire budget at that time was $18 million, the equivalent of a mere rounding error in the U.S. Department of Education's $63 billion annual budget.

The recipients are fairly typical of any large, urban school system—more than 80 percent are African American and most of the remaining kids are Hispanic. They live in the most marginal of neighborhoods. Average income is approximately $23,000 per year. Most are stuck in dysfunctional schools that are among the worst in the country. It should come as no surprise that the voucher program became extremely popular with the families of the recipients fortunate enough to be selected.

Amid this most hopeful of programs comes Eleanor Holmes Norton, the congressional delegate from the District of Columbia, who, in partnership with the Washington Teachers' Union, wished to end the program. The stated reasons in opposition are all too familiar to observers of the charter school and voucher debates: these programs drain money from traditional public schools and send a signal of resignation and defeat to the general public. A more complete answer would include the desire of the teachers' union to shut the door on all competition within its educational monopoly.

The sheer weight of the merits attached to the D.C. program is impressive. At the inception of the program, the $7,500 voucher was approximately one-half the $13,000 it took to "educate" a child in the District of Columbia. The district's traditional schools have been dysfunctional for decades despite one of the highest per-student expenditures in the country. Public charters, voucher programs, and homeschooling are more popular than ever as a result. And, finally, it appears a few within the political system are coming around to the notion that simply dumping ever-increasing tax dollars into failing schools is not the answer.

Enter Kevin Chavous, an African American Democrat on the D.C. City Council who decided in 2003 that, after years of staunchly opposing vouchers, it was time to introduce more choices in the city school system. In February 2003, Chavous decided "enough is enough"; he told a gathering of influential business leaders in Washington that a lot of money was not enough. "Public schools won't reform themselves internally," he said. "They will only respond to external pressures and a more educated electorate."[68]

---

[68] Spence S. Hsu, "How Vouchers came to D.C.," *Education Next* (4) no. 4, Fall 2004.

If only such an opinion could morph into the majority view in urban areas around the country!

Chavous must be congratulated for his change of heart; such actions are all too rare in those jurisdictions under staunch union control. But it took a realigning election to bring the D.C. scholarship debate full circle.

The pinball history of the controversial school choice program is a case study in support of the notion that elections do indeed have consequences: a Republican initiative circa 2004 to assist low-income D.C. students, a newly elected Democratic administration pulling the plug on new applicants in 2009, a soon-to-be Speaker of the House, John Boehner, reviving and expanding the program as part of a year-end budget deal in 2010, and an unenthusiastic President Obama signing off on the program's revival in recognition of a new political reality that began November 5, 2010.

The fortuitous election of a pro-voucher Speaker should not be the determining factor for providing many poor kids an opportunity to succeed. The implementation of life-saving, opportunity-laden programs should not be difficult. In more blunt terms, there must be a point at which the multigenerational failure of poor, urban school systems will lead to widespread civil rights activism within the community—not just the by now all-too-familiar calls for "more money." How long will single-digit passing rates be greeted with passive resignation, rather than a sustained demand for systemic reform?

The bottom line: taking on the education establishment's resistance to fundamental reform for the benefit of poor, disproportionately minority kids sentenced to failing schools will *always* be the right thing to do, even when such leadership is not rewarded at the ballot box. It may serve to touch a few heretofore hard-to-reach hearts and minds in the greater community, too. Of course, a far better solution is to reach heretofore difficult-to-touch hearts *and* be rewarded with new allies, political and otherwise. The emergence of a new generation of aggressive, progressive urban school superintendents around the country is a case in point. And none has proven more aggressive than former District of Columbia Public Schools Superintendent Michelle Rhee.

Rhee followed a hyperaggressive reform agenda during her tenure leading one of the most change-resistant school districts in the country. At any particular point in time during her tenure, she could be found closing underutilized schools, reforming a dysfunctional special education program, revamping a top-heavy central administration, or simply implementing intensive teacher development programs. Most importantly, she managed to raise expectations among parents and the press to the effect that real progress can be achieved within one of the more notorious school systems in the country. That she had done so in the face of open hostility from the D.C. teachers' union and, more recently, the U.S. Congress speaks to her relentless, indefatigable approach to the job.

In October 2010, Rhee resigned after her boss, D.C. Mayor Adrian Fenty, lost his bid for reelection. Rhee's firing of 241 teachers and decision to place an additional 737 on notice to improve within a year or be fired had been a critical issue in Fenty's loss to City Council Chairman Vincent Gray.

Rhee's departure after sustained and well-reported battles with the D.C. teachers' union and the Obama administration should not lessen our enthusiasm for what she accomplished, against long odds, and the fans she generated along the way. Ever incremental reform should be applauded when the worst of the worst is at issue. Here, any progress means another marginalized kid might just receive an opportunity to punch his or her life ticket—always a worthy and wonderful goal.

Taking On
Britney Spears and
Celebrity 'Role Models'

*"If I had an opportunity to shoot Britney Spears,
I think I would."*

— KENDEL EHRLICH

ONE OF PRESIDENT BILL CLINTON'S more memorable cultural
moments was his well-publicized condemnation of the black rap-
per Sister Souljah for her statement that "if black people kill black
people every day, why not have a week and kill white people?...So
if you are a gang member and you would normally be killing somebody, why not kill a white person?" Clinton's unexpected condemnation won him widespread praise from the left and right and was
somewhat remarkable in light of his well-recognized iconic status
within the African American community at large.

Perhaps then Vice President Dan Quayle's most memorable cultural speech took issue with a TV sitcom character, Murphy Brown, for having a child out of wedlock. Despite being made the focus of relentless attacks by late-night comics and other Hollywood intelligentsia, the vice president's persistent defense of the two-parent home and relentless jabs at the "cultural elite" won him widespread praise in the heartland. The criticism of a fictional character was part of the "family values" theme of the Bush-Quayle ticket of 1992. It also served to again thrust into the political debate the real societal cost associated with fatherless families—not a laughing matter to the millions of kids forced to grow up without a male role model in the home.

In 2000, Senator Joe Lieberman (D-CT) attacked Hollywood executives for the increasingly violent images directed at impressionable children. The comments as focused on the media elite were not a general warning either, as Lieberman threatened to have the Federal Trade Commission (FTC) use its fair and deceptive safeguards as guidance for the benefit of parents. The threatened action followed an FTC report that found evidence of increasingly violent and vulgar content being marketed to kids through advertising campaigns and other marketing venues.

Tipper Gore, wife of future Vice President Al Gore, triggered a controversial national debate in 1985 over sexually explicit lyrics with her proposal to require the music industry to place warning labels on records with sexual, drug-related, or violent content. Her purpose was to educate parents about the increasingly popular trend toward lyrics that were sexually explicit, glorified the use of drugs or alcohol, or were excessively violent. Of course, an aggressive public relations counteroffensive was launched by a variety of heavy metal bands, rappers, independent record labels, and First Amendment advocates. The theme: keep Tipper Gore's hands off our freedom of speech. The controversy led to a series of congressional hearings in 1985, which, in turn, led to a decision by the Recording Industry Association of America to place parental advisories on selected releases at its discretion. In the end, the effectiveness of the "Tipper Sticker" remains an open question, as some observers believe the presence of the stickers serves to make the product more attractive to impressionable young buyers.

The Power of Influence

These four story lines are examples of how four high-profile individuals used their status to positively engage on one or more fronts of the modern culture wars. Charging into the cultural battle is something the Ehrlich family knows about firsthand. Like these four influential people in government, a tall, attractive, media-savvy First Lady of Maryland was at the center of her own cultural controversy in 2003.

After my election as governor, Kendel knew exactly which issues she would focus on as First Lady: substance abuse and domestic violence.

Having served as both a public defender and a prosecutor, Kendel had been exposed to the most egregious examples of family dysfunction. In both positions, she observed cycles of bad behavior that revolved around the issue of why so many people ended up in court: most either dropped out of school, were addicted to drugs or alcohol, or both. She also observed how addiction often led to destructive and violent behavior that endangered spouses and children in the home.

In October 2003, Kendel was asked to speak at a conference of domestic violence workers, including victim advocates, in Frederick, Maryland. She was thrilled to have the opportunity to discuss her experiences in prosecuting domestic violence cases. After all, her audience was immersed in this topic, fighting it daily, and therefore would likely have constructive ideas for breaking the epidemic and saving lives and families. The best ideas always come from those on the front lines. Little did we know that this important talk would set off an astonishing chain of events.

Kendel knew her subject matter cold, as usual. As an assistant state's attorney, she regularly watched female victims drop domestic violence charges against their husbands or boyfriends because they feared for their safety or believed they lacked an alternative remedy. The fact pattern in these cases became all too familiar to her. First came a relationship that included episodes of physical abuse. These incidents in turn led to criminal charges and an initial court appearance. It was typically around the time of the court date that rapprochement occurred; quite frequently the abused party would show up for court hand in hand with her abuser. His assurances of future good behavior would not satisfy Kendel, but to no avail. She had no case with an uncooperative complainant. Many of the abused women Kendel saw at this time had little formal education, suffered from addiction of one form or another, and had children with one or more men. They simply concluded they had no better option. As a result, Kendel observed battered women leave behind a dignified resolution while returning to a dangerous relationship. Her experiences left her frustrated. "How can women allow themselves to get trapped in such abusive relationships?" she would ask me at home after a day at the courthouse.

She knew that part of the answer was to teach young women to respect themselves and, better yet, to become emotionally and financially independent.

Looking for Answers

As First Lady of Maryland, Kendel searched for solutions to domestic violence that transcended what could be achieved in the courtroom. She knew that part of the answer was to teach young women to respect themselves and, better yet, to become emotionally and financially independent. Kendel was raised by a stay-at-home mom who taught her that there's nothing wrong with a wife who decides to postpone employment and raise a family. Jane Sibiski also raised Kendel to value an education and secure all the skills needed to take care of herself and her family if life ever took a turn for the worse.

Kendel understood that teaching young boys to respect women was absolutely critical to fostering healthy relationships and strong marriages down the road. When we had our first son in 1999, Kendel and I agreed this last notion would be a bedrock principle in how we raised Drew.

So, as Kendel was introduced to her audience of domestic violence workers in October 2003, she knew what needed to be said. After speaking a bit about her career and the goals of my administration, Kendel set aside her prepared remarks and spoke bluntly with her audience about the negative influences she believed were so pervasive in the lives of our children:

> We have to ask ourselves, how we are raising our young women and men in the most advanced country in the world. We have to really examine ourselves and understand what young women are taught and who they are taught to look up to. This country is craving real and truly accomplished role models who can be examples of success. Instead, we teach our young teenagers to be influenced by celebrity and pop culture. We subject them to relentless marketing for skimpy clothing worn by Britney Spears. If I had an opportunity to shoot Britney Spears, I think I would.[69]

Kendel knew instantly that "shooting Britney Spears" may not have been the best choice of words, but the crowd loved it. They gave her a booming round of applause. Years in the courtroom had taught her to read her audience and, in this instance, the audience was enthusiastically on her side, and they clearly knew what she meant.

"I hate to say that," she continued, "but I am raising a boy, and I think, oh my goodness, what would I do if I had a daughter who is seeing these images and having peer pressure?"

Kendel finished her speech and never gave her comments a second thought. She most certainly did not mention her choice of words to me at home that evening. Two days later, the press began calling—and calling and calling.

By Monday morning, numerous national and international news organizations were contacting us about Kendel's comments. Sure enough, the press was all over her reported desire to kill Britney. "You have got to be kidding me," Kendel said to me. "Surely they know what I meant." Judging from the flood of calls, apparently they did not.

---

[69] Kendel Ehrlich, speech to Domestic Violence Prevention Conference, Hood College, October 3, 2003.

Topless (Almost) Britney

It would be helpful at this point to recall just where the trajectory of Britney Spears' career was when Kendel delivered her remarks. Britney had long since achieved pop-icon status. She was twenty-one years old, had just posed essentially topless for the cover of *Rolling Stone*, had routinely posed seductively on magazine covers before and after turning eighteen, and had recently kissed Madonna on the mouth before an international television audience. This was before Britney married, had the marriage annulled, married again, had two children, got divorced, flashed her private parts before a bank of cameras, reportedly checked into rehab, reportedly checked out of rehab, shaved her head, checked into rehab again (reportedly), and lost custody of her children.

CNBC—yes, the business network—was all over the "story" of Kendel's comments. Alan Murray said, "As the father of two daughters, I understand the sentiment about Britney Spears as a role model, but the notion of shooting her is rhetoric gone wild."

Sky News in England wrote, "Kendel Ehrlich, who is married to top politician Robert Ehrlich of Maryland, said the previously virginal singer should be punished for her latest raunchy look."[70]

A Google search by our press staff indicated that news websites as far away as Singapore had picked up the Britney story.

Kendel assumed a simple response to the flood of press calls would be appropriate, one that made clear she did not intend to (literally) shoot Britney Spears. Her office issued a statement to that effect, but it did not satisfy that insatiable appetite for anything associated with Britney.

The next morning, Kendel and I were jarred awake from the Britney sound bite on the morning news. Her comments actually beat out Arnold Schwarzenegger's election in California as the top news story of the morning.

That's when we knew it would not be a good day. For the only time in my tenure as governor, the reporters gathered outside the gates of the governor's mansion were more interested in interviewing

---

[70] "I'd Shoot Britney—Politician's Wife," Sky News, October 8, 2003.

my wife! As the press inquiries accumulated, Kendel and I sat down with my communications staff to determine how best to end the persistent coverage. You see, there is a caveat to the general rule on holding one's ground in the face of aggressive criticism—apologize when appropriate. Accordingly, Kendel decided she would hold a press conference that day and express her regret for using an inappropriate choice of words but stand firm on her underlying point: popular culture makes it difficult to raise confident, independent daughters, as well as sons who respect women.

Her comments actually beat out Arnold Schwarzenegger's election in California as the top news story of the morning.

Later that day, Kendel met the press at a previously scheduled charity golf tournament. Rest assured, the promoters of the tournament had no idea they would get this much media attendance. For the first time in her life, Kendel was in front of a massive bank of cameras on her own. She stepped up to the microphone and expressed her sincere regret for the inappropriate choice of words.

> It was off the cuff and in jest. And that's stupid when you're in public life, and I should know better. So it's a tough lesson, and it's not an easy lesson, but I think most people know that it wasn't meant in any literal sense at all.

Then, like any good lawyer, she pivoted her audience back to her central point.

> You have to look at how we're raising our young women and our young men, and specifically the influence of pop culture in that and how it just helps make it a little bit more difficult for parents.[71]

---

[71] Kendel made these remarks at a charity golf tournament in Queenstown, Maryland, on October 8, 2003.

Kendel also extended an invitation to Britney to visit Maryland and cohost a charity concert for domestic violence victims. (That invite was declined, in case you were wondering.)

Stick to Your Guns

Kendel's unplanned run-in with Britney reinforced a valuable lesson: when the message is important, stick to your belief system, even where you regret a specific word choice. The impressions our children carry into the world are too important to be left to the influences of unchecked celebrities. As parents, we must be willing to suffer a few bruises in order to draw the line for the sake of our kids.

It is parents who must lead if we are to turn this part of pop culture around.

A month later, ABC's Diane Sawyer sat down with Britney and asked for her thoughts on Kendel's comments. Britney told her, "Well, that's really sad that she said that. Eww. You know what, like, I'm not here to, you know, babysit her kids."[72]

She also told *Entertainment Weekly* that Kendel "probably needs to get laid."[73]

Well, with Kendel five months pregnant with our second son at the time, Marylanders got a good laugh out of that one.

To this day, Kendel continues to receive e-mails, letters, and unsolicited supportive comments about "the Britney incident." The vast majority are offered by parents of young girls—parents frustrated with pop culture's relentless targeting of young girls with messages of casual drug use and promiscuity.

Such images are not going anywhere soon. Commercial speech is free speech, and sex always sells in a free marketplace. It is parents who must lead if we are to turn this part of pop culture around. Only time will tell if enough parents in our busy world are engaged enough to subdue such negative messaging within our culture.

---

[72] Britney Spears, interview with Diane Sawyer, *Primetime with Diane Sawyer*, ABC-TV, November 13, 2003.

[73] Benjamin Svetkey, "All Eyes on Britney," *Entertainment Weekly*, November 13, 2003.

Taking On Our Business Community Allies

*"There is inherent in the capitalist system
a tendency toward self-destruction."*

—JOSEPH SCHUMPETER[74]

TURNING THE POLITICAL PRACTICES of the "politician class" around has been one of the most frustrating initiatives of my public life as a candidate and officeholder.

As a self-described pro-market, pro–free enterprise politician, I found that it was usually easy to defend the employer class against familiar, class warfare–driven attacks from the left. Why was it so easy? Because I never forgot the old adage that there are no employees without employers—so one better pay attention to who creates real jobs in the real world.

---

[74] Joseph Schumpeter, *Capitalism, Socialism and Democracy* (London: Taylor & Francis, 2003).

But my ideal road map for a private sector–focused, perpetual job-creating machine was not always realistic. Our ideas get turned upside down when we're confronted with the realities of interest-group politics.

Case in point: the Maryland gubernatorial election of 2006, where the aggressively pro-business Republican governor of Maryland received campaign donations from a handful of organized labor organizations, mostly law enforcement groups long aligned with my views on crime and punishment. The few thousand dollars raised from these organizations constituted a drop in the bucket when compared with the $17 million raised by my campaign.

This, of course, is not terribly surprising. Despite the decidedly conservative bent of many labor households, the propensity of organized labor leadership to lean exclusively left has been well established for decades. This contribution pattern shows itself up-ballot and down-ballot in races across the country.

The far more interesting and disturbing aspect of the modern money chase lies with the giving habits of the business community. These habits constitute a disquieting story and are the primary reason business communities in general find it so difficult to influence election results, let alone individual lawmakers. It is a story not often analyzed by the press but one that demands investigation by all who seek to understand why "influential" business interests so often fail to influence policy and politics.

Contribution records from our 2006 gubernatorial race illustrate the problem in glaring terms. My opponent, Baltimore Mayor Martin O'Malley, received contributions from business entities totaling in excess of $3.5 million. This despite the fact that he was aligned politically and philosophically against the interests of Maryland's businesses. Indeed, private sector and public sector union activists were transparently visible in positions of authority with the O'Malley campaign from Day One; no serious businessperson could claim surprise when those same union activists later became transition team leaders for a new labor-dominated administration.

Some of these dollars were donated by Baltimore businesses having contracts with the city of Baltimore. This is the way the fund-raising game is played. I do not approve of this practice, nor do I seek to condone it. I do understand it, in that there exists a direct link with the government contracts that keep many small businesses afloat. For larger context, check the political-contribution patterns of the so-called "Beltway Bandits"—small government-dependent consulting firms that have sprung up around the Washington Beltway over the past thirty years.

Far more embarrassing is the propensity of midsize and large businesses to provide funding for candidates who make it their practice to oppose business initiatives They are case studies in an easily intimidated business class regularly "shaken down" for contributions in order to cover all the bases. These businesses are often afflicted with the "Stockholm Syndrome," in which an imprisoned person or business begins, over time, to identify with his or her captor. I was intimately familiar with this practice given my experience in Maryland politics. Prior to my election in 2002, Maryland businesses had been so consistently beaten at the polls that these "insurance donations" had become part of the status quo. Accordingly, anti-business candidates expected this money to flow freely from the captured.

I had explored this theme in hundreds of speeches given during my tenure in Congress, because it applied equally to many business interests around the country. In 2001, I "dared" the Maryland business community to break out of this destructive behavior and truly support the business candidate for governor—me. We were able to achieve some success, as late-arriving business money bought the extra television ads against an energized Kennedy money machine during the last days of the campaign.

Pro-Business Governor

As governor, it was my plan to push for a more-even playing field for job creators, particularly for the smaller business owners often left without representation in the halls of power. Further, given the tenuous nature of our hold on the levers of power in such a blue state, and the strongly left-leaning Maryland General Assembly, I knew we had to strike quickly—and with a serious push.

And so, in April 2004, I spoke at the annual luncheon of the Maryland Business for Responsive Government, one of the few serious business groups on the right within the Maryland business community. It was not the number of members that gave the group its political power (it was relatively small) but rather the annual legislative scorecard that had forced more than a few suburban Democrats on the defensive when explaining anti-business votes to their check-writing and vote-casting constituents.

The annual luncheon is well attended by businesspeople, lawmakers, and members of the press. I saw this as a unique and very public opportunity to push the business community to finally take a stand in support of deserving members of the legislature—regardless of party affiliation—and against those who opposed opportunity and entrepreneurship. I arrived midday at the Baltimore Convention Center prepared to give the first in a series of public denunciations and challenges to the Maryland business community at large.

Rest assured, the seven hundred members of the business community in attendance that day were expecting anything but a denunciation. They had an unapologetically pro-business governor for the first time in a long time who had taken time out of his schedule to attend their luncheon and discuss the business community's new seat at the table in Annapolis. At least temporarily, life was good for them. They gathered inside the convention center for lunch, drinks, and to trade in the daily gossip permeating political and boardroom circles. But within just a few minutes of my opening pleasantries, I turned the mood of the room upside down.

"You have yet to prove a willingness to engage those members who enjoy your checks and your endorsements, but who vote at critical times against jobs and growth and opportunity and prosperity.... That's the Patty Hearst syndrome. You identify with your captors. The time has come for the Maryland business community to lose that syndrome."[75]

The room was quiet.

"I do not care how many e-mails are sent over ninety days. I do not care how much money you pay to powerful lobbyists in

---

[75] David Nitkin, "Ehrlich Scolds Businesses for Lack of Lobbying," *The Baltimore Sun*, April 23, 2004.

this room.... We need you to influence votes. We need you to be dangerous."[76]

Across the cavernous hall. the silverware and glasses stopped clinking.

"It is very quiet in this room right now, because this may not be the speech you expected to hear. I'm not going to sit down there [in the State House] for two more years as a backstop."[77]

For some, it was an unpleasant experience. Many surely expected the usual "'atta boy" approach from a proven friend. It was a call to arms to "get dangerous" for those who should have been engaged but had chosen the easy road of going along to get along. The press ran to the usual establishment types I had targeted for criticism. Their reaction was predictable.

"This is damning evidence that Bob Ehrlich has brought the very worst of Washington politics to Maryland," charged the Maryland Democratic Party. "The governor is changing the culture in Annapolis by endorsing the Washington tactic of using intimidation and bank accounts to hijack the people's agenda."[78]

At least the Democratic Party flack got it half correct. I wanted a direct confrontation with the leadership of the business community. And I wanted to make the conflict as transparent as possible in order to educate the membership as to the questionable behavior of the leadership. The "happy warrior" within me was thrilled to engage in this project for the benefit of my political base—the small business owners who did not have the time to walk the corridors of power because they were too busy running businesses. Once begun, I was enthusiastic that real progress could be made.

Within six months, the business community was showing strides. A wire story ran the headline, "Business leaders will reward friends, go after enemies." The Maryland Chamber of Commerce dubbed its annual legislative conference "Getting Dangerous." A good gauge of the efforts was the reaction by the leaders of Maryland's political establishment. Speaker of the House Michael Busch went so far as to

---

[76] Ibid.
[77] Ibid.
[78] Ibid.

warn the Chamber of Commerce against ranking lawmakers according to their votes for and against business interests. In other words, a threat was issued to the business community to be real careful about its newfound relevance and don't dare use actual votes on real legislation to hold us accountable!

From the outset, I realized that even under the best of circumstances, my campaign could only achieve partial success given the number of Maryland-based businesses dependent on local, state, and federal government contracts. These businesses will always seek to indulge and placate anti-business candidates for fear of offending the Democratic Party leadership—the group that is almost always in power in states such as Maryland. As stated earlier, these "admission price" contributions are easy to understand due to the source of dollars that keep the company in business. Nevertheless, these dollars represent opportunities lost for so many otherwise deserving candidates who would vote a pro-growth business line if given the opportunity.

Still others in the business community have limited stakes in government contracts, yet insist on salting the political landscape with contributions all around. The central objective is to guarantee "relationships" with those in power, even where those in power consistently vote or work against their interests. The occasional crumb from the leadership's table, usually in the form of a returned phone call or meeting, is enough to keep the contributions flowing. These are the most damaging dollars because the contributions are given simply to stay in the game and maintain access, regardless of the recipient's voting record.

My situation was unique in the annals of recent Maryland political history. Here was an unapologetically pro-business governor challenging the business community to defend itself, while that same community's antagonists answered by threatening retaliation if business decided to heed my call and expose the anti-business politicians of the ruling elite. That last statement was a mouthful, but it is much easier to read than to think about the utter weakness of organizations that fail to defend themselves, and the utter arrogance of political leaders who threaten, shout, and promise retribution to anyone who dissents from the monopoly's party line.

Case in Point: A Banker's Story

Ed Hale, one of Maryland's most prominent bankers, launched in 2003 what was intended to be a serious advocacy group for the business community in Annapolis. Hale and twenty other members of Maryland's business elite created the Maryland Business Council to, in their words, "represent, protect, and advocate for the often-neglected interests of business" in Maryland. The council's mere existence was an admission by the business community that Maryland's ruling elite had steamrolled their legislative priorities for years and that the state's established business advocacy groups weren't up to the task of turning the tide. An April 20, 2004, *Baltimore Sun* article was most encouraging in the context of Hale's promise to "fill a void."[79] Hale's most promising statement was his vow to use the newly formed group to "represent the previously underrepresented." I was so excited by this seemingly serious group that I agreed to speak at one of its initial conferences in front of a room full of business leaders at Towson University in April 2004. I gave the assembled a version of my "Get Dangerous" speech, in conjunction with an emotional plea to "help me, help you" in the unfolding battles with the General Assembly.

A promising first year marked by activism on issues ranging from tort reform to Big Labor's infamous "Walmart bill" provided a source of further encouragement. As the 2006 election year approached, however, and the polls reflected a tight race for governor, the council's public lobbying took a more passive course. When it came time to contribute to the campaign coffers of elected officials—the ultimate test of an advocacy group's seriousness—the council gave to just two candidates in the entire state: me and my anti-business opponent, who just happened to control the permitting process in Baltimore. It was the classic hedge bet.

The presidential election of 2008 provides a striking context. In that year, many of the major Wall Street investment houses led the fund-raising charge on behalf of the transparently anti-business Barack Obama. Top donors included Goldman Sachs, Citigroup,

---

[79] June Arney, "Maryland Business Council Launched as a Needed Advocate," *The Baltimore Sun*, April 20, 2004.

JPMorgan Chase, and Morgan Stanley. These and other giants of U.S. capitalism raised big money for the senator from Illinois with the lifetime United States Chamber of Commerce rating of 32 percent.[80] They celebrated his historic win in high style. For no apparent reason, they saw a new friend in the White House.

Fast-forward two years and the "smartest guys in town" are left scratching their heads, with some very publicly asking for a strong GOP nominee to take on the president.

So, what happened? Well, it seems a failed stimulus, historic deficit spending, calls for higher taxes, two liberal Supreme Court justices, and the National Labor Relations Board's declaration of war against right-to-work states, among other misdeeds, finally garnered their attention. One wonders what part of the prepresidential Barack Obama résumé led the Wall Street elite to such euphoric hopes in the first place.

Everybody loves to be with a winner, and the business community is no different. It has, however, a unique propensity to switch sides at the whim of a statewide or national trend. Again, this pragmatic approach may not generate goodwill or votes from hostile legislators, but it does let many business interests sleep at night thinking, "At least I can get my phone call returned," or, more tangibly, "My program—appropriation—tax preference will be preserved and protected." Conversely, examples of union-left or simply run-of-the-mill left-leaning groups pulling a similar switch to support conservative or business-friendly legislators is virtually nonexistent.

Indeed, despite what everybody knew would be a terrible midterm cycle for Democrats in 2010, left-labor groups continued to spend big money in support of their endorsed liberal candidates: 94 percent to Democrats and 6 percent to Republicans. *They* play to win. *They* typically will not pay protection money. *They* will compete hard against you even where their opportunity to knock you off is slim. Their dollars, endorsements, volunteers, phone banks, direct mail, and commercials reflect their serious approach to politics. If only a similar critical tide could be built and sustained by the job creators!

---

[80] Voting record of Barack Obama, Project Vote Smart website, www.votesmart.org/issue_rating_ category.php?can_id=9490 (accessed August 21, 2011).

Unfortunately, it is far more likely than not that the business community at large will maintain its status as a political front-runner rather than a political street fighter. Most larger business enterprises will continue to play the game the way it's always been played. Old habits are difficult to break. The ability of small and mid-sized businesses to forgo custom is a more realistic possibility. The more entrepreneurial, the more likely they are to resist ingrained sensibilities, particularly where the enterprise is not dependent on direct government contracts or subsidies. Given that every business must undergo some degree of government regulation, it is left to the individual owner to decide whether his parochial interests outweigh the benefits to be gained from support of an ideologically compatible candidate. My effort in Maryland was to reinvigorate the idea of "supporting those who support you," even when politically inconvenient, dangerous, or chances for success were minimal, because it is the only way to build an ever playing field against the increasingly anti-business agenda of the new left and its increasingly aggressive public union allies.

Special Session

Recent circumstances compel an additional footnote to the Maryland business community's limitless ability to placate the opposition when the pressure is on. (Please feel free to delete "Maryland" and fill in your favorite state's business community if the following story touches a nerve.)

The Maryland General Assembly was called into special session by my successor, Martin O'Malley, in November 2007. The alleged purpose of the meeting was to deal with a projected shortfall in the next fiscal year's budget to begin July 1, 2008. Among a number of poorly-thought-out new taxes was a brand-new sales tax on computer services.

The new tax took Maryland's large and growing technology sector by surprise. The inside word at the time had the General Assembly proposing to extend the sales tax to health clubs, tanning salons, and landscaping services—new services that would be added to the sales tax base in order to generate immediate revenue. There was no hint of any desire to capture computer services in a state boasting thousands of smaller technology companies in business to support the numerous federal defense and research facilities in Maryland.

As if by magic, however, in the late-evening hours of November 13, 2007, the governor and legislature included "computer facilities management and operation, custom computer programming, computer system planning and design, software and communication technologies, computer disaster recovery and data processing and storage and recovery, as well as hardware or software installation or maintenance and repair"[81] in a newly expanded Maryland sales tax base. Another bill added insult to economic injury by raising the sales tax from 5 percent to 6 percent. The net impact of the legislation was to impose a new 6 percent sales tax on computer-related technology services, delivering a potentially devastating blow to the backbone of Maryland's high-technology-driven economy.

Reaction was swift and negative. The Tech Council of Maryland, Maryland's largest technology trade association, took the lead. A January 15, 2008, news release announcing the council's 2008 policy platform listed one priority above all others:

> "TCM's 2008 Policy Platform focuses on a number of areas, but our members have been particularly outspoken against the recently instituted sales tax on computer services," said Julie Coons, Chief Executive Officer of TCM. "The complete repeal of the computer services sales tax is TCM's top priority," said Coons.[82]

Business groups large and small joined in a historic campaign to repeal the new tax. Surprisingly, newly elected State Comptroller Peter Franchot, one of the legislature's most progressive votes during a twenty-year career in the Maryland House of Delegates, joined the pro-business, anti-tax chorus: "We're urging them to take another look at this particular component of the tax package" was Franchot's not-so-thinly disguised criticism contained in a January 1, 2008,

---

[81] Andrew A. Green, "Legislators pass tax increases, spending reductions," *The Baltimore Sun,* November 19, 2007.
[82] Tech Council of Maryland, "Tech Council of Maryland Releases 2008 Policy Platform for Technology and Biotechnology," news release, January 14, 2008.

Washington Post analysis of the largest tax increase in Maryland history.[83]

The heretofore politically inactive information technology sector formed a new advocacy group to lobby for a computer tax repeal, the Maryland Computer Services Association. The association immediately began its public education campaign through news releases, media appearances, and a website. The foundation for the effort was the thousands of mostly small technology sector businesses that, by 2007, had grown to a collective sixty-eight thousand employees with a payroll in excess of $2 billion. The association's initial press release was quite explicit about the negative impact(s) of the new tax:

"Strategic investment in technology has long been the key to success for many of Maryland's leading industries, including bioscience, financial services, healthcare, higher education and government contracting," said Larry Letow, president and COO of Convergence Technology Consulting and a founding member of MCSA. "By levying a tax on their investments, Maryland is significantly hindering the ability of all Maryland companies to successfully compete in the global marketplace.... Created in response to Maryland's Tax Reform Act of 2007, MSCA's first order of business is the full repeal of Maryland's Computer Services sales tax."[84]

So, with the industry in full battle mode by the second week of January 2008, who do you think was the featured speaker at the Tech Council's 2008 "Leadership Dinner"? Well, none other than...Martin O'Malley! Yes, the same Martin O'Malley who had just supported and signed the most destructive piece of technology legislation ever passed in Maryland was the occasion's star attraction. The Tech Council could barely contain its enthusiasm in its press release announcing O'Malley's participation:

[83] Phillip Rucker, "Many of Md. Tax Increases Will Go into Effect Today," *The Washington Post*, January 1, 2008.

[84] Maryland Computer Services Association, "Maryland Computer Services Companies Join Forces to Urge Repeal of Tax Increase," news release, January 8, 2008.

The Tech Council of Maryland (TCM) is proud to announce that Maryland Governor Martin O'Malley will be the featured Keynote Speaker at the association's 2008 Leadership Dinner on January 22, 2008, at the Annapolis Marriott Waterfront Hotel.

This is the first time that Governor O'Malley has spoken to TCM members who are senior IT, biotechnology and corporate executives from throughout Maryland.

"This is one of the most important Leadership Dinners we have ever hosted," said Julie Coons, TCM Chief Executive Officer. "Our members will be able to hear first-hand from the state's chief executive. Governor O'Malley is a dynamic and engaging speaker and our members are anxious to hear from him."

Governor O'Malley is expected to speak about a host of compelling state issues including the state-of-the-state, economic priorities for technology, biotechnology, and the state's business climate moving forward. In addition, he is expected to talk about his administration's accomplishments and give a "from the top" forecast of the current legislative session.

The TCM Leadership Dinner is a members-only event held annually that allows the most senior executives from the association's member companies access to Maryland's legislative leaders. In addition to Governor O'Malley's speech, attendees will also be given a formal presentation on TCM's 2008 policy priorities.[85]

Welcome to my world. And, by the way, I was *never* invited to the AFL-CIO's annual legislative dinner. Same for the SEIU, trial lawyers, Emily's List, and...well, you get the idea. A brief footnote to an unfortunate idea: the infamous Maryland tech tax was repealed on April 3, 2008. What is not subject to repeal (or measurement) is the substantial damage inflicted on an already shaky Maryland business reputation. To paraphrase that old Chinese proverb—play with fire, get burned.

Is there any wonder why business lobbies find it so difficult to compete and win against their more-focused opponents?

---

[85] Tech Council of Maryland, "Governor O'Malley Is Featured Speaker at Tech Councils of Maryland's 2008 Leadership Dinner," news release, January 15, 2008.

Taking On the Attack against the Institution of Marriage

"Gay marriage is an oxymoron."

—Governor Robert L. Ehrlich, Jr.

ACTIVIST JUDGES OFTEN SEEK to create policy outcomes that legislators and the public oppose. This pattern of judicial activism has played itself out in any number of controversial social issues, including abortion and gun control. Today's "hot issue of the month" is marriage, and the culture warriors of the left have launched a relentless offensive aimed at the singular definition of marriage as a union between a man and a woman. The pattern has, by now, become familiar to all who follow the national debate over marriage.

The strategy calls for one or more gay "couples" to sue a resident subdivision clerk's office in order to secure a marriage license. In Maryland, a complaint was filed in 2004 against City of Baltimore

Clerk Frank Conaway seeking to overturn a 1973 Maryland statute that defined a valid marriage as limited to one man and one woman. In January 2006, a Baltimore City Circuit Court judge agreed by holding the 1973 law unconstitutional on the grounds it discriminated on the basis of gender in violation of Maryland's Equal Rights Amendment. The Maryland Court of Appeals (Maryland's highest court) subsequently ruled in a four-to-three decision that same-sex marriage was not a fundamental right and such policy decisions were more appropriately within the jurisdiction of the legislature, not the courts. The reaction from gay advocates was as expected—they would continue to fight for their "rights."[86]

For many people of faith, a concept clearly unthinkable twenty years ago is today a front-burner issue generating a tremendous amount of controversy within Christianity and Judaism—and additional acrimony within particular denominations.

So, what is the correct strategy and outcome for those who seek to protect the sanctity of traditional marriage *and* wish to bestow substantive rights on unmarried couples and even platonic friends who wish to care for one another in medical or end-of-life situations?

One aspect of the debate is clear for all to see: the relentless campaign to promote gay marriage from a variety of the usual suspects, including Hollywood scriptwriters, the American Civil Liberties Union (ACLU), increasingly aggressive gay rights groups, hyperactivist judges, and, for no apparent reason, organized labor.

These advocates use a variety of common, familiar tactics, including gay-oriented television and movie scripts (Hollywood), civil rights lawsuits (ACLU), political campaigns (gay rights groups), and support from more mainstream groups and associations associated

---

[86] In early 2010, an unexpected assist was provided by Maryland Attorney General Doug Gansler when he issued an opinion declaring that Maryland would recognize same-sex marriages executed in other states. The opinion required state agencies to provide gay married couples the same legal rights as heterosexual couples.

with traditional policy but willing to assist anyone or anything with an ideological agenda friendly toward left-leaning Democratic candidates (organized labor). These diverse groups have achieved rapid success in taking a onetime fringe issue and placing it into the mainstream of public debate: most recent national polls have only a slim majority of Americans opposed to gay marriage, with a clear majority of Democrats in support.

Not surprisingly, this broad and aggressive coalition has been assisted by the growing acceptance of gay marriage/civil union proposals by many mainstream Christian churches and reformed synagogues. For many people of faith, a concept clearly unthinkable twenty years ago is today a front-burner issue generating a tremendous amount of controversy within Christianity and Judaism—and additional acrimony within particular denominations.

My purpose is not to explore the fault lines on the issue of gay marriage within modern religious practice. Rather, it is to remind the reader that the mere *fact* of this heated debate points to the progress of the gay agenda within modern culture—and politics.

As with other sensitive social issues discussed in this book, the increasingly permissive nature of our American society must not stop a commonsense majority from placing yet another clear marker in the defense of culture. Congress did so in 1996 when it passed a law barring federal recognition of same-sex marriage and allowing states to do the same. I voted for the law and it was an easy vote for me: the clear goal was to protect traditional marriage. The rationale for this defense is clear: *if* traditional marriage is the cornerstone of our Judeo-Christian culture, and *if* the most constructive nurturing environment for children requires the presence of a male *and* female influence, and *if* we are serious about placing rational limits on the proliferation of behavior-based protected classes, then it follows that such a foundational institution must be protected and preserved.

The suppositions in the previous paragraph must be understood if the commonsense majority is to prevail over the long term. From a historical perspective, it is irrefutable that marriage between one man and woman is a cornerstone of the religious traditions upon which our country was built. The same is true for many religious traditions over the centuries.

Second, the importance of male *and* female role models in child-hood maturation is not only self-evident but it is also difficult to imagine any serious person holding a contrary view. Indeed, the government's rational interest in promoting a sound, functional environment for child-rearing and procreation was the basis of the Maryland Court's decision upholding traditional marriage.

Homosexual Parents?

It is at this point that an important caveat must be noted: I understand that same-sex couples are able to be good and loving parents.[87] My life's experiences have shown me it is not only possible but accomplished with increasing frequency today. Conversely, children require love, support, and socializing skills from *both* genders. Public policy preferences should follow suit. For example, dual-gender households should be given priority over single-gender households with respect to custody and adoption practices. In the real world, however, the number of children in need of loving homes is far greater than the number of traditional relationships willing to adopt. Accordingly, I do not advocate for the suspension or elimination of gay adoption. To me, it is simply not the *preferred* option.

My third element concerns the willingness of policymakers to create new categories of behavior-based protected classes under civil rights laws. This wide-ranging initiative has been the result of a sustained campaign by gay rights advocates to associate the gay rights/marriage movement with the civil rights movement of the 1960s. In legal terms, it marked a turning point because it signaled the expansion of protected class status to *behavior-based classes*. No longer would protected class status be limited to race, ethnicity, or sex. Now, certain behaviors like sexual orientation, weight, etc., would be brought under the umbrella of expanded legal protection. Further, the legal and policy consequences of expanded protected classes presents expanded opportunities for additional litigation—a

---

[87] Maryland courts have allowed members of gay households to serve as legally adoptive parents for years. This view is derived from a Maryland Court of Appeals decision holding that sexual orientation is not a relevant factor in determining what constitutes the best interests of a child in custody and visitation matters.

potential bonanza for trial lawyers, but not such a positive result for the many small businesses and consumers who will pay the freight.

The policy departure represented by behavior-based classes is important because it requires enhanced legal rights derived from protected class status to *follow* the behavior, i.e., an individual who practiced a gay lifestyle at one point in life but who subsequently became heterosexual would no longer be afforded protected class status.

This begs the ultimate issue underlying the entire gay marriage/gay rights debate: Are certain individuals born gay or is it a learned behavior? I decline the invitation to answer as I do not pretend to understand whether being gay is genetic or a choice. It may indeed be both. It is a matter of record, however, that some individuals change sexual preference during the course of their lives—some more than once.

The advent of behavior-based protected classes presents employers, employees, and lawyers with new and difficult challenges. These issues will be sorted out, at great expense, by the courts. The far more fundamental issue of what constitutes a marriage should not, however, be left to judges who seek to remake society and societal institutions through an ideological lens. It falls to the legislature (or to the people through referendum) to act in order to protect the culture at large.

> *Children require love, support, and socializing skills from both genders. Public policy preferences should follow suit. For example, duel-gender households should be given priority over single-gender households with respect to custody and adoption practices.*

Putting It in Perspective

A 2004 article by Kay Hymowitz in *City Journal* uses historical perspective to examine how gay advocates have advanced their case through association with the civil rights movement and appeals to a post-1960s generation sensitive to the importance of committed

The Ehrlich Family circa 2005.

relationships (possibly because they have been exposed to the family traumas brought about by the "anything goes" attitudes of the sexual revolution) and profoundly opposed to *any* form of discrimination. It follows that baby boomers and younger generations today possess a more sympathetic view toward gay marriage.

Hymowitz's point is well taken; this "sensitized generation" theory is as good as any I have researched in explaining the easy acceptance of generation Xers to gay marriage. The disconnect occurs with the issue of children, as Hymowitz explains in quite clear terms:

Are certain individuals born gay or is it a learned behavior? I decline the invitation to answer as I do not pretend to understand whether being gay is genetic or a choice.

What the young neo-traditionalists have trouble understanding is that their embrace of the next civil rights revolution, as many of them are inclined to see the fight for gay marriage, is actually at war with their longing for a more stable domestic life. Gay marriage gives an enfeebled institution another injection of the toxin that got it sick in the first place: it reinforces the definition of marriage as a loving, self-determining couple engaging in an ordinary civil contract that has nothing to do with children. That's no way for marriage to get its gravitas back. It is marriage's dedication to child rearing, to a future that projects far beyond the passing feelings of a couple, that has the potential to discipline adult passion.[88]

During my tenure as governor of Maryland, there was a legislative attempt to overturn the Circuit Court for Baltimore City decision that held traditional marriage unconstitutional. A Republican attempt to bring a constitutional amendment to the floor of the House of Delegates, which defined marriage as the union between one man and one woman, was quickly defeated on a procedural move in order to protect suburban Democrats from voting on the controversial

---

[88] Kay S. Hymowitz, "Gay Marriage vs. American Marriage," *City Journal*, Summer 2004.

issue during an election year. It appeared that even in Maryland there was a limit to how far left the Democratic leadership would trend with an election looming.

A medical registry act that would provide same-sex, unmarried heterosexual couples and platonic friends the same ability to make serious medical decisions for one another would fail to satisfy the real agenda.

My support for the constitutional amendment was met with harsh criticism from Equality Maryland Executive Director Dan Furminsky: "Anybody who endorses writing discrimination in the Constitution...is certainly not a friend to fairness and justice and the thousands of Maryland families who have a vested interest."[89]

And here lies the problem with so many of the gay activist groups who are unwilling to accept long-sought-after extensions of substantive rights (hospital visits, end-of-life decision making) because of their underlying goal of *remaking* the institution of marriage. Accordingly, my support for a medical registry act that would provide same-sex, unmarried heterosexual couples and platonic friends the same ability to make serious medical decisions for one another would fail to satisfy the *real* agenda.

California's Same-Sex Marriage

The campaign to radically redefine traditional marriage took a major, albeit temporary, step forward with the May 15, 2008, decision to allow same-sex marriages in California. Indeed, the dissenting opinion from California Supreme Court Justices Marvin Baxter and Ming Chin alluded to the "cataclysmic transformation" of marriage resulting from the decision. Baxter and Chin continued:

---

[89] Andrew A. Green, "Marriage Measure Rejected," *The Baltimore Sun*, February 3, 2006.

[A] bare majority of this court, not satisfied with the pace of democratic change, now abruptly forestalls that process and substitutes,
by judicial fiat, its own social policy views for those expressed by
the People themselves.

Baxter and Chin went on to quote the New Jersey Supreme Court:

We cannot escape the reality that the shared societal meaning of
marriage—passed down through common law into our statutory
law—has always been the union of a man and woman. To alter that
meaning would render a profound change in the public consciousness of a social institution of ancient origin.[90]

Of course, the subsequent failure of the gay marriage referendum
in California and other left-leaning states offers hope that the commonsense majority can be energized when it counts. Nevertheless,
the contemporary crack in the concept of one man–one woman
marriage will only widen as advocates look to other liberal-leaning
legislatures and state appellate courts willing to find rights in state
constitutions heretofore hidden from plain view.

The task ahead is easy to define but challenging to reach. Charges
of "insincerity," "homophobe," and "right-wing extremist" will ring
out wherever and whenever opposition to gay marriage unfolds.
Nevertheless, it is essential for candidates, officeholders, and opinion leaders to lay the proper predicate before a purely negative image
of traditional marriage advocates becomes engrained in the minds of
younger voters. Indeed, Hollywood's incessant campaign to mainstream gay values through movies and television places all culture
warriors on the defensive. In light of the challenge, the silent su-
permajority needs to act—now. And "action" in this context is to define what is at risk if same-sex marriage becomes the law of the land.

First, it is appropriate that we articulate again and again the widely accepted proposition that government has a quite limited interest
in consensual behavior between adults. Americans tend to be zeal-
ous protectors of their privacy interests; most accept the premise

---

[90] In Re Marriage Cases, 43 Cal. 4th 757 (2008).

Governor Ehrlich and his wife hoist their son, Drew, as he gives two thumbs up on Election Night 2002.

that government's role of "moral policeman" is indeed limited where legal adult behavior is at issue.

Second, overt moralizing, even on an essentially moral issue, will not win the day in the court of contemporary public opinion. Those for whom gay marriage is an abomination already oppose the concept. For those who follow the mantra of "live and let live," the rational reasons for the protection of traditional marriage, especially the two-gender influence on child development, must be articulated in artful ways, without the heavy moralizing from the right that has, at times, marked the public debate and given plenty of added fuel to gay marriage advocates.

Third, hundreds of conversations over the years with gay friends, staffers, and colleagues have convinced me what may not be obvious to most—that there is a difference of opinion within the gay community as to how far to push the issue of gay marriage. For some gay Americans, it is *not* a primary policy issue. To the extent individual gay, conservative voters are "in play" on social, economic, or international issues, why not attempt to make the point that opposition to gay marriage is not a signal of opposition to everything or everyone gay?

Finally, it is the rather large group of American adults who carry a freedom-loving, libertarian bent but also worry about the coarsening of the culture who are the true majority makers on this issue. Ultimately, it is they who will decide whether marriage as we have known it since the beginning of time will survive. The case in support of traditional marriage is a strong one. We should not allow the rapid liberalization of so many of our cultural norms to discourage us from a blunt, rational approach to a commonsense majority presumptively supportive of this cornerstone institution.

Taking On
the Failing War on Drugs

"How much easier it is to be critical than to be correct."

—BENJAMIN DISRAELI

IN 2003, MARYLAND RANKED THIRD nationally in the percentage of state prison admissions for drug offenses, according to a study by the Justice Policy Institute, a national group that advocates for alternatives to incarceration. At the time, approximately 25 percent (5,750) of Maryland's twenty-five thousand inmates were incarcerated on drug offenses and as many as 85 percent entered prison with addictions or related substance abuse problems.

Maryland, like so many other states, was condemning too many young offenders to the adult criminal justice system through long incarceration and without substance abuse treatment. The overrepresentation of younger substance abuse offenders in the adult system was partially a result of the "get tough on drugs" policies that swept through state legislatures in the 1980s and early 1990s. A popular policy initiative at that time was to increase the predicate offenses through which young, increasingly violent drug offenders were "waived up" to adult courts—and to adult sentences. The failure to even attempt breaking the familiar cycle of addiction (offense, incarceration, reentry, and subsequent offense) meant that our recidivism rate would remain far too high, with little political motivation to do anything about it.

Project Diversion

Any observer of contemporary American society understands the disproportionate impact of this vicious cycle on young African American males. Overrepresentation of this subgroup in our juvenile and adult prisons is the subject of much political debate, and a powerful issue within the larger African American community. I was well aware of this sense of resentment dating back to my time in the state legislature as I observed members of the Legislative Black Caucus of Maryland engage in lengthy, emotional attacks on the then increasingly popular notion of mandatory minimum sentences for drug-related offenses. I wanted to funnel this outrage into support for a uniquely Maryland approach to the plague of drug abuse. And so, from Day One of my tenure as governor, I stressed the importance of diverting nonviolent drug offenders out of the criminal justice system and into treatment programs, where they belong.

In 2004, I put my words into action. I authored and won passage of an alternative to incarceration for nonviolent offenders. The legislation, commonly referred to as "Project Diversion," made it easier for qualifying drug offenders to obtain treatment instead of jail time.

Project Diversion created the first-ever state-structured diversion system for prosecutors to use in nonviolent offenses through "*nolle prosequi* for drug or alcohol treatment" or "stet for drug or alcohol treatment." In practice, this means a prosecutor can decline prosecution (*nolle prosequi*) of a case or place the case on an inactive, or stet, docket to enable a qualified offender to secure drug or alcohol treatment. If the offender successfully completes treatment, he can petition to clear his or her record in three years. An offender can only qualify if the state health department or its approved drug or alcohol abuse evaluation determines the offender is amenable to treatment.

The limitless nature of our drug problem also requires action behind prison walls. Accordingly, my legislation provided assistance to offenders in prison seeking parole; Project Diversion required the Maryland Parole Commission to consider a drug or alcohol evaluation when determining whether an offender was suitable for parole. An offender who was amenable to treatment and not serving time for a violent or major drug distribution offense could be released on parole prior to serving one-fourth of his sentence in order to undergo appropriate treatment.

Project Diversion has helped to change the way Maryland's justice system views substance abuse problems through a more holistic, cost-efficient, and effective approach to overcoming the drug addiction epidemic. I knew our bill struck the right balance when one of my staunchest opponents from the 2002 election recognized this "commitment kept."

In April 2005, hip-hop mogul Russell Simmons told WBAL-TV in Baltimore, "I campaigned against [the Ehrlich-Steele ticket], but he made a certain commitment to communities.... The economic empowerment ideas he had, the reform of criminal justice system—especially in terms of drug laws—a lot of people have given lip service about these ideas, but they came in and they've lived up to them."[91]

Programs such as Diversion make sense for younger, nonviolent offenders in need of additional services. But what about the thousands of addicts already in the system? The vast majority will reenter society at some point in time, a fact often lost on some pundits. In many cases, these addicts return to the streets as addicted as when they originally entered the system. It should come as no surprise they reoffend in large numbers. Currently, Maryland's adult recidivism rate stands at 49 percent.[92] Research has shown that, nationwide, up

---

[91] "Hip-Hop Mogul's Message on the Money for Youth," WBAL-TV, April 21, 2005.

[92] Nancy S. Grasmick and Thomas E. Perez, "Correctional Education and Re-Entry," in the *Workforce Creation and Adult Education Transition Council Report*, December 2008, www.dllr.state.md.us/adulted/aereport (accessed August 23, 2011).

to 67 percent of those released are rearrested within three years,[93] creating a cruel and increasingly expensive cycle of incarceration.

Thirty-second attack ad–centric political campaigns rarely touch upon this inconvenient fact: when individuals do reoffend, they not only produce new crime victims but also cost taxpayers additional money by rejoining an increasingly overburdened criminal justice system.

Lack of access to substance abuse treatment is only one barrier awaiting those leaving prison. Inmates are often ill-prepared to return to the community, lacking access to cognitive-skills training, employment readiness, job opportunities, affordable housing, parenting skills, and social service resources, all critical elements for an individual's successful reentry and continued reorientation into the community.

In addition to helping individuals stay on the right path and reducing crime, these programs also save significant taxpayer dollars and ease the financial burden on the states, too.

As governor, I was committed to seriously confronting the cycle of incarceration, and, in four years, Maryland became a national leader in prison reform. After reviewing a major national study conducted by the Washington State Institute for Public Policy, which found that the best reentry programs could deliver 20 to 30 percent reductions in recidivism, and that even modest reductions in future criminality can have an attractive bottom line, I was intent on bringing the reentry philosophy to Maryland. Again, this goal was not necessarily in response to demands from my conservative base, nor did it generate much praise from my detractors on the left. It was simply a recognition of what challenges needed to be addressed—and funded.

---

[93] U.S. Bureau of Justice Statistics, "Two-Thirds of Former State Prisoners Rearrested for Serious New Crimes," news release, June 2, 2002.

Reentry Programs

Effective reentry programs reduce recidivism and make our communities safer. They should be the focal point of any serious reform effort. In addition to helping individuals stay on the right path and reducing crime, these programs also save significant taxpayer dollars and ease the financial burden on the states. A Philadelphia Prisons System report on that city's corrections system showed that by reducing recidivism rates by just 10 percent there would be a savings of $6.8 million in jail costs alone. From 1982 to 1997, state spending on incarceration increased from $9 billion annually to $44 billion, and that does not include the cost of arrest and prosecution. The annual cost of adult incarceration in Maryland is $24,000 per inmate. This is three times more expensive than the annual tuition at our flagship state school, the University of Maryland at College Park.

Project RESTART

No program illustrates our administration's aggressiveness better than "Project RESTART," a system for offender reentry that had not previously existed in Maryland. It is an approach that balances custody and control with treatment services, providing offenders with the tools necessary to become contributing members of their communities.

RESTART, an acronym for "Reentry Enforcement Services Targeting Addiction, Rehabilitation, and Treatment," is not rocket science. It is practical; it makes sense. It contains four major program components—correctional education, substance abuse treatment, social work, and offender reentry—and is based on numerous research studies that emphasize the importance of cognitive restructuring programs, academic training, vocational skills training, and substance abuse treatment in reducing recidivism.

Although legislative budget cuts (often instituted by lawmakers who had previously advocated for such a program under Democratic administrations) limited the number of prisons where RESTART was implemented, the strategy added new programming in pilot institutions that research has demonstrated to have a positive impact on recidivism.

An inmate, in a 2006 petition for clemency, wrote, "Idle hands are the devil's playground. Every day I watch people who wander aimlessly, just waiting to be drawn into something—bad or good." This individual succinctly summarized why Maryland and every other state should expand on the RESTART strategy—ensuring prison programming is targeted to diminution in violence. Only then will we observe more successful offender reentry and reintegration.

It means policymakers can become ever more aggressive with their ideas, if they can show progress is possible and if they can successfully remind everyone that the "lock 'em up and throw away the key" road we have followed for so long has failed—at great expense.

It is a reality that offenders are the parents, siblings, and children of those who live in our communities, and they can either enrich or impoverish those lives when, not if, they return home. During my four years in charge of Maryland's criminal justice system, I made it a priority to assist these families and communities by helping those behind bars "be drawn into something...good." We made progress, but so much more must be done throughout our criminal justice system.

One final note about the politics surrounding programs such as Project Diversion and Project RESTART pertains to the willingness of conservative audiences to accept such cutting-edge ideas. Not so long ago, the conventional wisdom held that this type of approval would be a nonstarter in white, suburban neighborhoods. Advocates were typically viewed as "soft on crime," a career-killing label in districts I represented in the state legislature and U.S. Congress. For context, the successful GOP attack on Bill Clinton's "midnight basketball" initiative comes to mind.

Today, there is much less trepidation surrounding such advocacy because so many families of all stripes have been impacted by the scourge of drug abuse. What was once viewed as that "urban problem" is now universally recognized as an "every family problem," crossing all lines of race, creed, ethnicity, and religion. This recognition took place gradually over the space of many years; it means that politicians with nontraditional, blunt views can be heard in politically costless ways. It means policymakers can become ever more aggressive with their ideas, *if* they can show progress is possible and *if* they can successfully remind everyone that the "lock 'em up and throw away the key" road we have followed for so long has failed—at great expense. It means that more conservative states can be as aggressive as we were in Maryland in their approach to drug policy. It may be a useful tool in improving race relations, too.

Maybe, just maybe, a more blunt conversation about the realities of drug abuse can lessen the racially charged nature of this issue. A parent is a parent, regardless of skin color. Those wide-eyed parents I observed in so many suburban audiences were no different from the wide eyes I observed in urban settings. Every parent shares the same fear about drug addiction. This mutual bond, born from mutual fear, can be a strong connector for a dialogue between the races. It only needs a bit of practical political leadership to push the connection forward.

Taking On
Medical Marijuana

"Cautious, careful people, always casting about to preserve their reputation and social standing, never can bring about a reform. Those who are really in earnest must be willing to be anything or nothing in the world's estimation."

—SUSAN B. ANTHONY

SOMETIMES, TAKING ON THE ESTABLISHMENT means "turning around" accepted views within your own party. These episodes do not occur on a regular basis but can be extremely painful, particularly where heretofore core values are reexamined under the glare of our 24/7 news cycle. On rare occasions, it means challenging traditional views and stepping on important toes, which is as good a way as any to introduce my position on medical marijuana, one of the hotly contested criminal justice issues of recent vintage. It is also an issue that tends to split traditional conservatives from the libertarian

167

right, let alone more liberal interest groups that have advocated for wholesale reform of our marijuana laws for many years.

As a member of Congress, I had been one of only a handful of libertarian-leaning members on right-to-die–related issues. Such a stance was not new ground for me: a willingness to run against the traditional grain on issues of individual liberty had punctuated my congressional tenure. It seemed to me that, short of assisted suicide, Republicans should adopt a commonsense, "hands-off" approach to this most personal of decisions: the federal government should not interfere with states' interests wherever possible, and the states should not interfere with individual citizens wherever possible.

> *Republicans should adopt a commonsense, "hands-off" approach to this most personal of decisions: the federal government should not interfere with states' interests wherever possible, and the states should not interfere with individual citizens wherever possible.*

On drug war strategy and the specific issue of medical marijuana, I clashed with what has come to be known as conventional Beltway Republican wisdom, a view that interprets our cultural drug epidemic as more a problem of supply, rather than demand. Accordingly, it makes no exception for medical necessity or the Tenth Amendment, that wildly inconvenient law that seeks to preserve for the states any rights not specifically granted to the federal government.

The conventional wisdom also ignores a most inconvenient fact—that the federal government was currently providing marijuana from its own production sites to patients who had been recognized by the courts as legitimately in need of treatment.

For many of my Republican colleagues in Congress, however, it was seen as a camel's nose under the tent, a first step toward decriminalization of a gateway drug. Hence, a position wholly unacceptable to most of the party's socially conservative base.

The constituents who were interested in my position received a blunt policy letter outlining my support for the idea and my desire to see less federal government activism on an issue I observed to be more within the jurisdiction of state legislatures. In fact, I pointed to my congressional cosponsorship of H.R. 2592, "The States Rights Medical Marijuana Act," which prohibited the federal Controlled Substance Act from overriding state law in cases where marijuana could be prescribed or recommended by a physician for medical use as a commonsense, federalist-friendly approach to the issue. Unsurprisingly, the Republican-controlled Congress never brought the bill to the floor for a vote.

Further, I was not bashful about expressing my views in public, although not a great deal of attention was paid to my independent position—at least while it remained one of 435.

Compassionate Use Act

Things changed dramatically after I was elected governor, as Maryland took up the issue of medical marijuana during the 2003 session of the General Assembly. The legislation, known as "The Darrell Putman Compassionate Use Act," had been introduced in the House of Delegates. The bill sought to provide judicial discretion to reduce but not eliminate criminal penalties for use of marijuana under certain medical circumstances. The measure allowed a person charged with possession or use of marijuana to introduce evidence related to medical necessity and, upon conviction and a finding of medical necessity, limited the maximum punishment to a fine of one hundred dollars. At the time, Maryland law allowed for a penalty of up to one year in prison and a thousand dollar fine for a possession offense.

Interestingly, the bill was sponsored by a number of conservative Republicans and liberal Democrats, including the House Republican minority leader. The bill passed the House seventy-three to sixty-two; it passed the Senate by a margin of twenty to sixteen.

The approach contained in the Darrell Putman bill did not exactly place Maryland on the cutting edge, either. At that time, twenty-three states had laws relating to medical use of marijuana; many had been passed through popular ballot initiatives. The laws passed in Alaska, Oregon, Nevada, and Washington exempted patients from criminal penalties where marijuana use was found to be under the supervision of a physician.

Political pressure to oppose any type of medical marijuana bill began to build as the controversial piece of legislation was winding its way through the legislative process. The opposition was led by the White House and John Walters, the head of the White House Office of National Drug Control Policy. Walters had used particularly harsh language in lobbying the General Assembly to defeat the bill, characterizing it as a "cynical, cruel, and immoral effort to use the sick and suffering." After the bill passed and made its way to my desk, the language became even more emotional, as Walters compared medical marijuana to "medicinal crack."

The lobbying campaign was further enhanced when Bill Bennett, one of my favorite political commentators, called to add his voice to the veto crowd. Even veteran members of my congressional staff who understood my long-standing position began to doubt the wisdom of signing the bill. How, they asked, would signing the bill jibe with our administration's "tough on crime" policy approach? In other words, why antagonize a friendly administration and a significant part of our political base over an issue that would never attract enough crossover voters to matter?

In reality, though, despite the Bush administration's power play and the expectation of significant criticism within certain conservative circles, the decision to sign the bill was not difficult. It reflected a long and strongly held view. My predisposition was well known and had only grown stronger watching my strong and athletic brother-in-law endure a painful final two months of life due to a wildly aggressive case of colon cancer. End-of-life decisions are always difficult and emotional; for the most part, government should keep its long arm out of these intensely private decisions.

Politics Versus Protecting Medical Marijuana Patients

I was the first Republican governor to sign a bill seeking to protect medical marijuana patients from jail, but it was never my intention to pick a fight with the Office of National Drug Control Policy. Nor did I feel it was my role to provide political cover to the president's ideological critics. My political agenda was a policy agenda to implement positions consistent with our administration's philosophical approach to government. I was not surprised, however, when Robert Kampia of the Marijuana Policy Project in Washington, D.C., observed that "Maryland's elected officials have rightly rejected the position of a hostile White House and drug czar, who believe that marijuana-using cancer patients should be incarcerated like common criminals."[94]

Added Erin Hildebrandt, a medical marijuana patient and mother of five from Smithsburg, Maryland, "Crohn's disease used to leave me too sick to ever get out of bed...until I discovered that marijuana helped me more than any medicine I had ever tried....It is John Walters who is 'cruel, immoral, and cynical,' not the people working to protect patients."[95]

It appeared to me that overheated political rhetoric on marijuana law reform was not the sole property of the right or the left!

To me, one of the most satisfying aspects of the medical marijuana episode was the degree of attention my stance generated at public appearances for many months after I signed the bill into law.

Quite often, an emotional "thank you" was accompanied by a story about a relative, spouse, or friend who had suffered through an agonizing death due to persistent pain that had proved impossible to control. Such anecdotes brought back memories of my brother-in-law's painful journey and only strengthened my resolve to speak out on the issue. As a general proposition, public opinion, as articulated to me in very public ways, seemed to support just about any end-of-life treatment beneficial to a terminally ill person.

I never missed a chance to remind the dissenters on my staff about this public reaction, too. Every politician loves to be proven "correct," or at least receive approval for a position taken on a highly controversial issue. But there was more to these reviews than the usual "attaboys" regularly received from political supporters—and

[94] S. A. Miller, "Antidrug Activist Says She Was Barred from Signing," *The Washington Times*, May 26, 2003.

[95] Bruce Mirkin, "MPP Defeates [sic] White House Drug Czar in Maryland Senate Passes Limited Protection for Medical Marijuana Patients," FreedomWriter.com, March 26, 2003, www.freedomwriter.com/issue26/am31.htm (accessed August 23, 2011).

some political detractors. Maybe it was a real surprise to some that a Republican would advocate for such a position. Maybe it was a sense of gratitude for others troubled by an emotional end-of-life decision. Maybe it was the political intrigue generated by a Republican at odds with the White House and drug czar that made for good copy. It was also a reminder that not backing down when friendly forces oppose you is as satisfying as staying tough when your enemies seek to tear you down.

CHAPTER FOURTEEN

Taking On the
Criminal Justice System

*"I have often found that mercy bears richer fruits
than strict justice."*

—ABRAHAM LINCOLN

IN 1995, MY PREDECESSOR in the governor's office, Parris
Glendening, announced that he would deny parole to all offenders sentenced to life with the possibility of parole, so-called "lifers," unless they were very old or terminally ill. Under Maryland
law, the governor has the sole authority to approve the release of
lifers. From 1997 to 2001, the legislature tried unsuccessfully to
overturn Governor Glendening's policy. In 2001, the Maryland State
Commission on Criminal Sentencing Policy recommended the governor consider each lifer's case individually. This effort was supported by one of Maryland's strongest victim advocates, Roberta Roper,
who had lost her daughter to murder and who told *The Washington
Post* in 2001, "I don't think we can ever make one sentence or one

decision that would be appropriate for everyone.... One size doesn't fit all."[96]

For eight years, Glendening's blanket policy blocked clemency for lifers unjustly convicted and unfairly sentenced to terms of confinement disproportionate to their involvement in the charged offenses.

Over the course of my twenty years in elective office, public safety had been a priority issue. As governor, despite an extremely tight budget situation, I committed the resources of my administration to make Maryland safer, including an aggressive prison construction program and a unique, targeted crime initiative that pumped millions of dollars into local crime prevention grants. Thus, as a general matter, I did and do not support parole for most violent offenders; rehabilitation has its realistic limits.

With all this in mind, however, as a candidate for governor in 2002, I promised to reverse Glendening's blanket policy of refusing to consider any lifer cases, and instead vowed to review each clemency request on a case-by-case basis. I kept this promise by establishing a comprehensive investigatory process to exercise my constitutional, statutory, and moral responsibility, while preserving public safety and enhancing criminal justice.

My investigatory process commenced with a full review by the Maryland Parole Commission, the state agency charged with investigations from which recommendations are made to the governor on pardons, commutations of sentences, and parole of people sentenced to life. After receiving the commission's recommendation, my Office of Legal Counsel conducted its own investigation, marshalling the full range of facts and viewpoints, including prosecutors' and victims' opinions. Moreover, petitioners were subjected to a battery of risk-assessment tests, a psychological evaluation, rigorous cross-examination by my attorneys, and, in some cases, polygraph examinations. My Office of Legal Counsel then presented each case, with its recommendation, to me for further deliberation and review.

All told, I commuted the sentences of five lifers, paroled six inmates who were terminally ill, and pardoned hundreds of mostly

---

[96] Maureen O'Hagan, "When Life Means Life; Without Parole, Md. Confronts Costs, Questions," *The Washington Post*, May 21, 2001.

minor offenders. Without question, the commutations of life sentences were among the most difficult decisions I made as governor. Each decision was fraught with political consequences; there was never a drumbeat in my political base for such an aggressive use of the executive power. I still remember the looks of angst from Greg Massoni, my press secretary, who was tasked with having to answer for my decisions at public press briefings. My constant reminder to Greg and other members of my senior staff who reflected Greg's sense of trepidation was that we were engaged to do what was right, not necessarily what was popular or easy.

Examining Maryland Cases for Possible Pardons

A typical set of facts and circumstances surrounding a commutation case may be the Arvinger murder from 1964.

Walter Arvinger was nineteen when his freedom was taken away. He was, by his own admission, on the wrong path, hanging with the wrong crowd. He committed burglaries with his friends when they came upon "targets of convenience"; auto theft was a popular side activity. In 1968, he was arrested in the beating death of James R. Brown.

At trial, the evidence demonstrated conclusively that Arvinger did not wield the weapon, a baseball bat, used to kill Brown. Witnesses also offered conflicting testimony about whether Arvinger was part of a group that planned to rob Brown. Nevertheless, after a one-day trial, he was sentenced to life in prison.

In 1998, the Maryland Parole Commission recommended Arvinger's release to Glendening. At that time, he had served more time in prison than his codefendants, including the defendant who perpetrated the murder. By the time I reviewed his petition for clemency, filed by a team of law students at the University of Maryland School of Law, he had compiled a positive record of institutional adjustment, including a continuous twenty-five-year run without a single infraction and a five-year incident-free period of work release.

On November 29, 2004 after much consideration, weighing the evidence against him and his request for fairness, I commuted

Arvinger's life sentence to "life suspend all but forty-five years with conditions," which made Arvinger a free man that very day.[97]

Through my clemency initiative, I kept the system tough: I denied clemency to twenty-three inmates sentenced to twenty-five years without parole under a "three strikes" law, sixteen lifers, six inmates seeking parole for medical reasons, and five inmates seeking holiday commutations. Yet I also brought a sense of balance: I personally considered seventy-two commutation cases and, in addition to the five lifer cases, granted three commutations of sentence to inmates sentenced to twenty-five years without parole, commuting their sentences to a term of years. The clemency system was in working order again.

A person convicted of conspiracy to distribute marijuana just once may find years later he is ineligible for student loans or a good job, regardless of having demonstrated both law-abiding and responsible behavior over a period of many years.

In a similar, yet less complex way, my next challenge was to put my gubernatorial pardon powers to appropriate use. The collateral consequences—the postsentence burdens—of convicting a criminal are extensive, affecting family life and representing lasting and permanent obstacles to employment, access to government services, citizenship, and full participation in civic life. These burdens often impose harsher and more sustained penalties than the actual criminal sentence. For example, a person convicted of conspiracy to distribute marijuana just once may find years later he is ineligible for student loans or a good job, regardless of having demonstrated both law-abiding and responsible behavior over a period of many years. His chances of working as a registered nurse or electrician could be all but dashed. After having a family, he may find he is permanently ineligible for participation in his children's recreational sport leagues. In short, good people who make mistakes in life but later mature, rehabilitate, and prosper can

---

[97] Executive Order no. 01.01.2004.69, State of Maryland (November 29, 2004).

be permanently stigmatized, thus becoming members of a disenfranchised class of Americans.

Few realize the number of people who possess criminal records. They might be our neighbors, coworkers, high school classmates, friends, or family members. Approximately one in four adults in the United States—more than sixty-five million people—have a criminal record.[98]

The governor's pardon power is the one significant mechanism for granting postsentence relief to people with criminal records. It absolves the recipient from the penalties and eliminates the burdens imposed by law for their conviction. From 1994 to 2003, only 134 people in Maryland benefited from this form of relief.[99] As a result, the Maryland Parole Commission, the state agency charged with compiling pardon applications, amassed a backlog of more than four hundred applications, effectively rendering a pardon inaccessible.

Here again, as a candidate for governor in 2002, I promised to review each petition for pardon, commutation, or parole on its merits. By August 2003, after evaluating best practices in other states and consulting with some of the nation's clemency experts, my "Executive Clemency Initiative" began in earnest. I implemented monthly meetings to personally examine approximately twenty clemency cases, which were first reviewed by the Maryland Parole Commission and then thoroughly investigated by my Office of Legal Counsel, headed by Jervis S. Finney, one of my mentors and a former United States attorney. I realized from the beginning that we had the opportunity to correct injustice, restore dignity, create hope and opportunity, and transform futures. No system of government is perfect, and the criminal justice system is no exception. In my view, executive clemency needed to have an operative role in Maryland's criminal justice system.

---

[98] Michelle Natividad Rodriguez and Maurice Emsellem, *65 Million Need Not Apply: the Case for Reforming Criminal Background Checks for Employment*, The National Law Project, March 2011.
[99] John Wagner, "O'Malley Is Far Behind Ehrlich's Clemency Pace in Md.," *The Washington Post*, June 21, 2009.

Governor Ehrlich on the stump in support of more sensible criminal sentencing laws.

Innocent People behind Bars

Michael Austin reinforced my view in a compelling way. In 1975, a Baltimore jury convicted Austin of killing a Crown Food Market security guard, Roy Kellam, by shooting him in the chest. After spending twenty-seven years behind bars for a crime Austin did not commit, Baltimore City Circuit Court Judge John Carroll Byrnes ruled in December 2001 that "no reasonable juror" would have found Austin guilty. Three eyewitnesses had said the triggerman was five foot eight and light-skinned. Austin is six foot five and dark-skinned. A key witness who later testified that Austin was not present at the time of the murder was never asked to testify at the original hearing. A time card that could have shown he was at work just before the murder went missing, and his attorney, whom a judge later declared "woefully ill-prepared," never called a supervisor to verify his alibi.

On October 31, 2003, I announced my intention to pardon Austin, absolving him from his 1973 wrongful convictions for murder, grand larceny, and handgun violation.[100] He served more than twenty-seven years in prison for crimes he did not commit. I recall telling *The Washington Post*, after I announced my decision, that Austin's case may have been the most egregious miscarriage of justice I had ever seen.

The overwhelming majority of my pardons, however, were not to people convicted of murder or other violent crimes. Hundreds of people legitimately convicted of relatively minor crimes, such as shoplifting, drug possession, and battery, offered compelling reasons for pardons. These people had served their sentences and demonstrated, many over the course of decades, remarkable turnarounds and productive lifestyles.

I remember one case in particular, a woman who applied for a pardon for five misdemeanor theft convictions, from 1993 to 1996, all drug-related, because she wanted to pursue a career in social work. She had overcome a serious narcotics addiction and was clean for eight years at the time she applied. She had become a lead facilitator for Narcotics Anonymous, a motivational guest speaker at the Maryland Correctional Institution for Women in Jessup, Maryland, and a sponsor of six women in their recovery from drug addiction. Additionally, since her offenses, she had earned a master's degree in special education from The Johns Hopkins University and in social work from the University of Maryland at Baltimore. She was the perfect social worker candidate, a person who overcame significant challenges to lead a responsible life and who was now willing to help others find the path to success and rehabilitation. All that stood in her way were her decade-old offenses, which were no longer

---

[100] Office of the Governor of Maryland, "Governor Ehrlich to Grant Clemency to Twelve," news release, October 31, 2003.

representative of the person she had become. This pardon recipient had *earned* my help, as did hundreds of other Marylanders.

In total, I reviewed 444 pardon cases and granted 228 of them. As a result, on August 25, 2006, *The Washington Post* stated that I was "prolific in granting clemency."[101] The Sentencing Project, a non-profit organization that promotes reduced reliance on incarceration and increased use of more effective and humane alternatives to deal with crime, declared Maryland under my clemency program as one of its "Models for Administration of the Pardon Power in the United States" and ranked the state as one of the "13 Most Active Pardon States" in the country. For the first time in my life, I was likened to an icon of the Hollywood left. Margaret Colgate Love, former United States pardon attorney for presidents George H.W. Bush and Bill Clinton, wrote in a paper: "It appears that the only two incumbent chief executives who approach their pardoning responsibilities with any amount of proper respect are Governor Robert Ehrlich of Maryland and President Josiah Bartlet of 'The West Wing,'"[102] referring to actor Martin Sheen's character on NBC's hit White House drama. This recognition of my effort was fun, but far more rewarding were the letters of thanks sent to me from successful citizens who now had that stain removed from a transgression that transpired long ago.

Our road map must account for human frailties—sometimes serious frailties—but also for the millions of individuals who overcome obstacles, turn their lives around, and transform themselves into productive citizens.

In four years, working with a great team of attorneys, I revived the clemency power in Maryland. Hundreds of people benefited, as did a state that saw its scales of justice reach a more equal and appropriate balance.

---

[101] Matthew Mosk, "Ehrlich prolific in granting clemency," *The Washington Post,* August 25, 2006.
[102] Ibid.

Take This Idea National

Unfortunately, our administration's record has proven to be more anomaly than rule, as executives of all stripes and ideological persuasions adopt a "hands-off" approach to clemency practice. Indeed, my Democratic predecessors and successor have manifested benign indifference to this gubernatorial prerogative. In this regard, the infamous attack ads that followed the pardon of Willie Horton so long ago (ads produced by both Republicans and Democrats) continue to haunt even progressive executives otherwise predisposed to follow an aggressive clemency program. When all is said and done, they understand that one bad call in a high-profile case could cost them an election.

Nevertheless, this state of things is unacceptable if we are to become a more just society. Our road map must account for human frailties—sometimes serious frailties—but also for the millions of individuals who overcome obstacles, turn their lives around, and transform themselves into productive citizens. It is incumbent for governors and presidents not only to understand this fact of life but also possess the political fortitude to restore lives. A just society demands it.

CHAPTER FIFTEEN

Taking On the Fiscal Crisis and Public Pensions

"I, however, place economy among the first and most important of republican virtues, and public debt as the greatest of the dangers to be feared."

—THOMAS JEFFERSON
in a letter to William Plumer, July 21, 1816

ON MAY 24, 2011, Democrat Kathy Hochul captured a GOP-leaning seat in upstate New York's Twenty-Sixth Congressional District. The victory brought unbridled glee to the Democratic Congressional Campaign Committee (DCCC), the group charged with electing House Democrats. This particular victory, however, created a more profound giddiness among Democratic House operatives because of the campaign's frontal attack on the House Republican budget blueprint offered by Rep. Paul Ryan (R-WI), a blueprint that cuts entitlement spending and a "gift" the DCCC hopes will keep on giving through Election Day 2012. As Nancy Pelosi would no doubt concur, those thirty-second attack ads on Medicare almost always seem to work. In fact, "Mediscare" is always the preferred tactic in any class warrior's handbook.

This state of things is good for House Democrats looking to win back a majority but not so good for the country. You see, the federal budget deficit is monumental and getting worse by the millisecond. The primary driver is uncontrolled entitlement spending, a prime target of the Ryan plan. And Americans of all partisan stripes have only recently begun to sit up and take notice.

So, how dire is the budget crisis? How out-of-control is entitlement spending? What will it take to regain control of our fiscal situation?

A cursory review of easily found budget nuggets reveals the following series of unfathomable facts:

- If the government began repaying the national debt at a rate of $10 million a day it would take approximately 3,800 years to pay it off.[103]
- Our national debt is increasing by roughly $4 billion every day; the government is borrowing approximately $2.63 million every minute.[104]
- The 111th Congress added more to the U.S. national debt than the first one hundred U.S. Congresses combined.[105]
- The U.S. government's debt-to-GDP ratio will hit 100 percent this year. The ratio was 62 percent in 2007.[106]
- The last ten debt limit increases have averaged $799 billion.[107]
- As of August 23, 2011, the U.S. national debt was $14,642, 479,577,182.00. That's fourteen trillion and change.

---

[103] Michael Snyder, "17 Shocking Statistics About the National Debt You'll Wish You Didn't Know," *InvestingAnswers.com*, January 7, 2011, www.investinganswers.com/a/17-shocking-statistics-about-national-debt-youll-wish-you-didnt-know-2097 (accessed August 23, 2011).
[104] Ibid.
[105] Ibid.
[106] Tom Lauricella, "Debt Hamstrings Recovery," *The Wall Street Journal*, June 27, 2011.
[107] Rep. David Schweikert, "The Last Debt-Ceiling Debate America Will Ever Have," *The Washington Times*, July 1, 2011.

How much is a trillion? Consider:

- If you were alive when Christ was born and you spent $1 million every single day since, you still would not have spent $1 trillion.
- If today you began spending one dollar per second, it would take you thirty-one thousand years to spend $1 trillion.
- One million seconds will tick off over the next twelve days; one trillion seconds will pass in 31,688 years.
- A trillion ten-dollar bills, taped from end to end, would wrap around the globe more than 380 times. That amount of money would still not be enough to retire the federal debt.

An emotional debate over this dismal state of affairs foreshadows each and every battle royale over raising the debt limit, but the rhetorical temperature reached a new high during the latest and greatest debt limit showdown of August 2011. This historic battle replayed the familiar, high-stakes game of budget "chicken" the American public has been exposed to over the past three years.

We have seen this movie before: Republicans make very public vows that *this* will be the very last such increase allowed without draconian budget cuts, while Democrats take to the airwaves in order to beat the GOP up for its negligence in placing the creditworthiness of the United States at risk. And at least with regard to this latest budget showdown, the nation's credit rating *really did* hang in the balance.

So, why is it so difficult to balance the federal budget at a time when both parties are allegedly desperate to do so?

My service on the U.S. House Budget Committee and as a House deputy whip leads to one simple conclusion: it's all about a constant pressure to spend. Fact: most human beings want approval; most elected officials crave it. Result: it is nearly impossible to control the primal urge to spend taxpayer dollars, or, more precisely, pile up gargantuan debt on the federal credit card.

A typical workweek in Congress may include visits by those advocating on behalf of victims of childhood disease, highway contractors, local elected officials, green-energy lobbyists, education advocates, or any one of tens of thousands of other well-intentioned, organized groups. On most occasions, the visits are respectful. The proposed spending is all about moving the proverbial ball forward. The pitch, of course, includes the most used, and abused, admonition ever: "a little money (investment) now will save more money in the long run."

Any serious reform must contain a hard cap on all discretionary spending going forward and the initial steps toward entitlement reform, including raising the retirement age and providing less generous Social Security benefits.

This spending culture has been the accepted fabric of congressional life for many years, regardless of partisan control.

But 2010 changed the political landscape in dramatic fashion. Nearly 20 percent of House members are freshman Republicans determined to get our fiscal house in order. And their promise to deliver now collides head-on with the aforementioned interest groups.

Cut National Institutes of Health orphan-disease funding? Explain that to the parents of a six-year-old with a rare form of cancer.

Cut highway funds? Explain that after the next catastrophic bridge or tunnel failure.

Cut community block grants? Explain that to your local mayors and county executives as local potholes deepen and senior centers close.

Cut tax credits for wind and solar power? But doesn't everybody want "clean and green," and energy independence?

Cut Pell grants? What kind of heartless politician denies poor kids access to a college education?

You get the point. Cuts impact real constituencies—groups of voters who desire a balanced budget but not at the expense of *their* favorite program or tax preference. You see, so many constituencies have come to depend on their piece of the federal pie.

Further, the politics of "yes" enjoys specific constituencies, and those constituencies are increasingly well organized. The politics of "no" is only recently in favor and enjoys only a generic, albeit large, constituency. Alas, large numbers of budget hawks rarely show up at the polls in consecutive cycles.

One other problem: the election cycles of 2006 and 2008 swept into power many members who possess a sincere philosophical bent to spend. Despite their reduced numbers, they believe in a large welfare state. They desire higher taxes. They are class warriors and Tenth Amendment detractors. They did their thing for four years…and they are betting that the politics of "yes" will again carry the day in 2012.

Long-term solutions have been in short supply during the present crisis. We citizens, however, have a right to expect real progress. Although "real" in this context may be difficult to articulate, any serious reform must contain a hard cap on all discretionary spending going forward and the initial steps toward entitlement reform, including raising the retirement age and providing less generous Social Security benefits.

Regardless of philosophical predisposition, there remains the fundamental question of whether the sheer size of the deficit has finally become so tangible that our familiar, institutionalized spending practices can be controlled.

Spending can be controlled, but only if the dire state of our budget crisis has been brought home to enough taxpayers that our collective addiction to federal dollars and tax preferences can be reined in at last. And this long-delayed reining-in will only be accomplished through a mutual, determined effort by the legislative and executive branches. Most likely, it would require monumental cooperation between a Republican president and GOP Congress with enough "Blue Dog" Democrats in the mix to complete a comprehensive fix of our federal budget woes.

An appropriate addendum to the list of budget tasks that need to get accomplished in the short term concerns the heavy policy lifting required to implement state pension reform. And here, quite unlike the bipartisan dysfunction on federal entitlement reform, there is progress being made in any number of state capitols around the country.

The public sector pension–generated trials and travails of Governors Scott Walker (R-WI), John Kasich (R-OH), and Chris Christie (R-NJ) have blazed headlines across the country for the better part of 2011. But my setting is Maryland, circa 2010, as I decided to again take on the most powerful political forces in Maryland—this time on the emotional issue of public sector pensions.

My thought process was sound, or so I thought. Why not say what needs to be said, in order to do what needs to be done, in the context of a national reawakening about sagging tax revenues and steadily increasing public sector pension obligations? Was this not what the tea party revolt was all about? Had not the serial overpromising of benefits to increasingly powerful public sector unions *finally* become a political liability? Could even deep blue Maryland, where one in three workers is employed by the federal, state, or local government, join the growing national chorus in support of public sector pension reform?

State Pension Obligations

The end of 2009 and early part of 2010 brought unwelcome news to state capitals—the mortgage crisis–induced Wall Street crash had, in turn, revealed an approaching tsunami of state pension obligations. The serial budget crises that followed hit the most poorly managed states and municipalities the hardest. In California, a $21 billion deficit by mid-2009 required Governor Arnold Schwarzenegger's administration to issue IOUs when it temporarily ran out of cash. The IOUs and additional speculation about the potential of the state defaulting on its debt obligations were a direct result of a well-analyzed, incredibly lucrative series of benefit packages passed by the state legislature in prior years when state contributions could be minimal and stock market investment gains were healthy.

In Maryland, the state pension obligation approached $35 billion, with unfunded liabilities of $14.7 billion out of a total liability of $14.8 billion for state retiree health care alone. A February 2010 Pew Center report on each state's pension fund liability found that Maryland was one of only seven states to receive zero points in Pew's grading system because it so underperformed. As a result of this newfound, "unwelcome during a campaign year" story line, the press and general public were beginning to ask uncomfortable questions. First and foremost, how would a new Ehrlich administration deal with the realities of unfunded pension obligations while maintaining a promise of no new taxes? And, from a candidate's perspective, how would we discuss the dire need for pension reform with Maryland's public sector employees while simultaneously asking for their vote?

The menu options were not attractive: increase the retirement age, roll back previously provided benefits, reduce benefits for newly hired workers, increase employee contributions, eliminate cost-of-living adjustments, and the granddaddy of them all—end defined benefit plans in favor of private sector–type defined contribution plans, or 401(k)s. Nevertheless, the time had come for some plain talk on pensions. The true cost of all past pension promises had to be a focal point for public discussion. And what better time as pension woes in California, New York, Illinois, and Greece filled the daily news cycles with ominous stories of empty coffers, worried public employees, and angry taxpayers?

There was one rather obvious political motivation at work, too. I needed to get ahead of the public education curve in two important respects. First, I needed to make state employees more cognizant of the looming crisis—an exceedingly difficult task given Maryland's political makeup and legislative track record. Second, I had to further strengthen the notion that the usual "go-to" option of yet another tax increase was not on the table. This, of course, was contrary to the usual Annapolis modus operandi, which is to continue to postpone action until the only option left is a tax increase.

In this regard, Maryland's political establishment had acted upon its looming pension crisis in a classic way. The tortured history that follows would make even the most cynical political pundit blush.

Task Force Created

In 2005, during my third year as governor, I signed into law a bill to create the Task Force to Study Retiree Health-care Funding Options. The bill required an actuarial valuation of the liabilities associated with Maryland's retiree health insurance obligation since new accounting rules required states to include obligations generated by postemployment health benefits to be reflected on state financial statements. The commission was also assigned the task of identifying policy options and associated costs for addressing unfunded health care liabilities.

The task force completed its job in a timely fashion and published its report in November 2006. Interestingly, one of the commission's major recommendations was to create a second commission in order to further study future funding options. Accordingly, during the 2006 session of the Maryland General Assembly, a second commission was created—this time a "blue-ribbon commission," presumably to separate itself from the original, generic commission. With 2006 being a statewide election year, the General Assembly made sure the report date would create no embarrassing recommendations. In fact, the new report date was postponed to December 31, 2008, a full thirty months of additional study and deliberation.

I realized that moving in a 401(k) direction was not an immediate panacea for a system facing massive unfunded obligations, but I also understood such a change targeted to newly hired state workers would make the system more predictable and lower the state obligation over time.

The newly created, high-powered commission then did...nothing. It held its initial meeting in August 2007, a full fifteen months into its term. The full dimensions of the looming problem must have struck home during that fateful first meeting, as the commission requested *another* year's extension in order to generate its final report. Alas, even this extension was not enough for our blue ribbon group—the December 2009 "final" deadline passed without a new report. And, yes, 2010 was a gubernatorial election year in the state of Maryland. So, with no controversy, the General Assembly again extended the due date for a final report to December 2011. For those scoring at home, the various extensions mean a final report will be issued five years from the creation of the second, "blue-ribbon" commission.

The glacial pace of reform is made possible only where an issue lacks immediacy and an easily salable remedy. For context, witness the failure of Social Security reform at the federal level. Similarly, in Maryland, there was little legislative motivation to remedy a problem that had no tangible short-term impact and remains exceedingly complex. The legislative filibuster that followed came as no surprise. Fear of political consequences carried the day. The familiar lesson is clear: if a problematic issue gains traction, just create a study commission. Better yet, a series of study commissions. This mere act mitigates short-term damage because it appears proactive and serious. Then postpone real remedial action to some point in the distant future. Make it a problem for future administrations. And if and when that time ever arrives, just pass a tax increase and tell the voters you did your best. At least in dark blue states, there will rarely be negative consequences at the ballot box.

Nevertheless, the Ehrlich campaign of 2010 charged headlong into the anticipated breach—and the reviews were as anticipated.

The arena was a highly anticipated *Washington Post*–sponsored debate against Martin O'Malley in October 2010. A wide range of questions from a three-person panel of journalists came fast and furious, but Maryland's fiscal challenges remained the prime topic of conversation. During the course of articulating what remedial action my administration would take to combat a looming multibillion–dollar deficit, I stated what so many other observers knew: "The era of defined contribution is here and everybody knows it."[108] The next day, a *Washington Examiner* headline captured the moment: "Ehrlich Stings Unions with Pension Plan." My purpose was not to sting anyone, but rather to substantively define what had largely been left unsaid in the heat of the campaign. I realized that moving in a 401(k) direction was not an immediate panacea for a system facing massive unfunded obligations, but I also understood such a change targeted to newly hired state workers would make the system more predictable and lower the state obligation over time.

It was a bold move but one I had hinted at throughout the campaign. It was a position sure to stir the union pot. And, I hoped, it was the type of honest appraisal expected by those aggrieved taxpayers

---

[108] Hayley Peterson, "Ehrlich Stings Unions with Pension Plan," *Washington Examiner*, October 15, 2010.

who had been agitating for fiscal reform and budget transparency in such large numbers all over the country.

Reaction proceeded upon ideological lines. On the one side was Blair Lee, a highly respected columnist for *The (Maryland) Gazette*. This son of a former Democratic governor was forever grateful whenever a Maryland politician spoke out against the politically correct Annapolis monopoly. In a pre–Election Day editorial endorsement, Lee made an impassioned plea for budget sanity and for yours truly:

> During the campaign, Bob Ehrlich took a huge risk by telling us that we can't have it all, that the state can't continue living beyond its means... [Ehrlich] called for reforming the state's $15 billion pension deficit by putting new employees on a defined contributions plan. O'Malley ducked the issue by deferring to yet another commission "studying" the problem. If Ehrlich wins he'll cut spending; if O'Malley wins he'll raise taxes... If you think we're undertaxed and that bigger government and more spending are the answers, vote for O'Malley. If you think that government, like the rest of us, must adjust to the "New Austerity," vote for Ehrlich.[109]

These and other supportive statements from like-minded budgeteers could not surmount the usual liberal orthodoxy from the likes of *The Washington Post*, whose editorial board wrote of its appreciation for "O'Malley's refusal to rule out new taxes," while dismissing my fiscal positions as "tilt[ing] disingenuously towards his party's anti-tax orthodoxy."[110] No surprise here. A few weeks earlier, my otherwise pleasant *Post* editorial board meeting had turned icy when the discussion veered to deficits and taxes. I understood that my failure to budge on taxes meant no repeat endorsement from a group otherwise unimpressed with O'Malley's intermittent board visits over the years.

---

[109] Blair Lee, "The Case for Ehrlich," *The (Maryland) Gazette*, October 22, 2010.
[110] Editorial, "Mr. O'Malley for Governor," *The Washington Post*, October 17, 2010.

Political Battles

The political dramatics surrounding my willingness to engage on pension reform got more emotional as Election Day drew closer. And, not surprisingly, it was the Maryland State Education Association that led the clarion call to defeat my reform agenda. This was the union that did not bother to interview me before endorsing O'Malley during the spring of 2010. Its leadership was mightily upset when I won in 2002, and they were again pounding the pavement against the worst of all possible worlds—a Republican governor living outside their political pockets.

In an October 15, 2010, speech to the union's assembled delegates, Executive Director David Helfman discussed a nationwide "assault" and "unprecedented coordinated attack" by conservative reformers bent on reducing member benefits through new defined contribution plans.

> The most severe changes have been in states shifting away from defined benefit plans to defined contribution plans, shifting all investment and longevity risk to our members. This pattern established by other states is being used to justify the same thing in Maryland. Delegates, when investment markets drop 25% in a single year, there's plenty of time for the state to recover. The same can't be said for individual educators. A shift away from defined benefits is a direct assault on educators and retirees. It's wrong, and must be stopped.[111]

Later, after castigating board members of the Maryland Public Policy Institute, a small free market think tank I had joined in 2007, Helfman got to his bottom line.

> MSEA Delegates, I've used the term *assault* several times during my remarks. I chose it deliberately. Anyone taking the time to examine the links among the conservative policy groups, newspaper

---

[111] David Helfman, speech at Maryland State Education Association Representative Assembly, October 2010.

staffs, and politicians who then read the statements they have made about our pension benefits, evaluation systems, school funding, and privatization understands that *assault* is *the* appropriate term. I know that MSEA is up to this challenge. There are three ways you can ensure victory. 1. Dedicate yourself to win this election in 18 days. There's no doubt that we're better off with Martin O'Malley as Governor.... Bob Ehrlich has made it clear. He did not want our endorsement. He never completed a questionnaire or interview. He's told us that he does not share our values, our objectives, our opinions. And yesterday... he announced in the debate that he would move to end defined pension benefits for all future educators. The choice in this election is *crystal* clear.[112]

> *The gargantuan nature of the debt burden also creates a sense of fear in the average voter; the enormity of the liabilities causes a sense of trepidation precisely because the obligation is so difficult to understand. In other words, though we may not fully understand the problem, we realize it is really bad and getting worse by the second.*

Reform Proposal from the Left

As an interesting footnote, a 2011 O'Malley reform proposal offered up in the face of increasingly dire pension-related obligations was met with bipartisan criticism. The tepid proposal offered employees a choice of either increasing their contribution rates to maintain current benefits or continue current contributions in exchange for reduced benefits. Newly hired employees would have a retirement age of sixty, rather than fifty-five. To no one's surprise there was no proposal to exit defined benefit plans.

The "gutsy" tactic undertaken by our 2010 campaign failed to generate enough votes to win the election. It may have backfired in such an overwhelmingly union-controlled blue state. Regardless

---

[112] Ibid.

of outcome, however, it was the right thing to do. For the first time in anyone's memory, it was becoming almost fashionable for politicians to offer up pension reform packages. And many of these reform packages contained provisions that would push newly hired public employees to join defined contribution plans.

All taxpayers have a stake in serious pension reform. As Carla Fried, a former senior writer at *Money*, has written, "We are all in this mess together."[113] The good news: what heretofore was toxic is now becoming the subject of serious debate. The bad news: the mammoth numbers involved in coming to grips with the problem.

A recent paper by two business professors, Joshua Rauh of Northwestern University and Robert Novy-Marx of Rochester University, places total state unfunded liability obligations at between $2.5 and $4 trillion.[114] Of course, any debate that speaks to trillions of dollars is beyond the comprehension of most adults. Eyes glaze over at the mere mention of such figures. Yet the gargantuan nature of the debt burden also creates a sense of fear in the average voter; the enormity of the liabilities causes a sense of trepidation precisely because the obligation is so difficult to understand. In other words, though we may not fully understand the problem, we realize it is *really* bad and getting worse by the second.

What to Do Now

So what do we do, now that what has been a proverbial third-rail issue has become an appropriate topic for public debate? First, continue the public dialogue along the lines of a new conventional wisdom—that progress must be made to secure benefit reform now. The new predicate: less-generous public sector pension packages will emerge from this near-death experience. The new benefit mix will be different across states, but the new denominator will most assuredly be a significant reduction in pension benefit levels.

---

[113] Carla Fried, "2011: The Year Public Pension Plans Get Whacked," MoneyWatch, CBS.com, December 10, 2010, http://moneywatch.bnet.com/economic-news/blog/daily-money/2011-the-year-public-pension-plans-get-whacked/1875/#ixzz1VspH4HzQ (accessed August 23, 2011).

[114] Joshua Rauh and Robert Novy-Marx "The Liabilities and Risks of State-Sponsored Pension Plans," *Journal of Economic Perspectives* 23, no. 4 (2009): 191–210.

Similarly, a new state employee paradigm will emerge in which retirees will gain more control over their investment options. A more significant worldview change will emerge as well: the notion of living off a one-size-fits-all, government-guaranteed defined benefit plan will gradually recede into history. This much-maligned transformation has already occurred in the private sector, where sympathy for state employee unions desperately trying to hold on to their guaranteed benefit plans runs shallow. Although these changes equate to additional volatility for retirees and difficult political decisions for politicians, the ultimate result will be more freedom—never a bad result in America.

Taking On the
Myth of Bipartisanship

*"The question we ask today is not whether our government is
too big or too small, but whether it works.... The nation cannot
prosper long when it favors only the prosperous.... [To] those
nations like ours that enjoy relative plenty, we say we can no
longer afford indifference to the suffering outside our borders;
nor can we consume the world's resources without regard to
effect. For the world has changed, and we must change with it."*

—PRESIDENT BARACK OBAMA,
inaugural address, January 20, 2009

THE MEDIA OFTEN BEMOANS, "Why can't we all just get along?"
But this simple plea misses the primary point of our combative
political system: elected representatives are supposed to stick up
for the ideals and ideas they championed during their campaigns.
Accordingly, why would anyone expect their elected leader to

indulge or placate those who seek to inflict bad policy solutions on the America we know and love?

If President Obama has his way, you won't recognize the government, the free market system, or, frankly, America as you once knew it. His admonitions and his audacious policy goals demonstrate very clear motives: equalize, discourage dissent, and become a nation of apologists.

Look at what we've gotten from him so far:

- the proposed closing of Gitmo;
- a trillion-dollar, pork-laden spending spree;
- calls for tax increases on the "rich";
- a historic credit rating downgrade;
- activist federal judges;
- increasingly intrusive regulators;
- a return to a "blame America first" foreign policy (so well described by Ambassador Jeanne Kirkpatrick during the Jimmy Carter era); and
- a wholesale government takeover of the American health care delivery system

These are but some of the extraordinary policy initiatives the Obama administration has brought to the front burner of American politics. Remember, too, this is just the beginning. As he gears up to fight for a second term, he'll promise more hyperaggressive initiatives for a bewildered country.

It should come as no surprise that the mainstream media has managed to characterize these and other policy initiatives as a "moderate course." Some may actually buy into this notion, but most disinterested observers see it for what it is—an attempt to market hard-left ideas in a softer light in order to generate a cult of personality based on mass appeal. Fortunately, this modus operandi is rather easily exposed, as moderates and conservatives daily challenge this agenda in newspapers, on talk radio, and in the blogosphere.

Yet "can't we all just get along" continues as the media's primary mantra. A related and far more dangerous notion is the idea that the Obama issues agenda is somehow "postpartisan," or that challenging the Obama agenda exposes one as a partisan during a time the American public allegedly demands a "bipartisan" political environment.

Of the two, the concept of a postpartisan environment is the most dangerous and the most easily dismissed. Although it may sound really good when you say it quickly, postpartisan means the end of partisan opposition. What could be more un-American than a plea to cease criticism of the ruling elite? The commencement of single-party rule will follow. Sort of like the old Soviet Union...or present-day Maryland.

If President Obama has his way, you won't recognize the government, the free market system, or, frankly, America as you once knew it.

Of course, some bloggers and commentators on the New Left wished all this were true, and that the election of Obama not only forever tarnished the GOP "brand" but that it also somehow ended the Republican franchise permanently. The realigning election of 2010 ended that pipe dream, but even the strong Democratic cycles of 2006 and 2008 left plenty of Republicans in Congress and thousands more in state and local offices throughout the country. Most had profound philosophical differences with the president, Speaker Nancy Pelosi, and Majority Leader Harry Reid. In many cases, these substantive policy differences did not lend themselves to bipartisan compromise. Instead, they led to clear-cut policy confrontation, from health care to stimulus to trade—and the GOP minority stuck to its guns. At times, especially when joined by moderate Democrats, they carried the day. Witness how fast candidate Hillary Clinton and then New York Governor Elliott Spitzer changed course on driver's licenses for illegal aliens once a commonsense majority of New Yorkers became energized on the issue.

A snapshot of right-center political activism brings the reality of a healthy loyal opposition into greater focus: the 2010 midterm election, the extraordinary strength and stability of conservative talk radio, the proliferation of market-oriented think tanks, the increasing popularity of action-oriented groups such as Americans for Prosperity, the success of "tea party" activism, and the cable ratings

domination of Fox News are not easily dismissed. All are ideologically motivated from the traditional or libertarian right. All have gained
strength since the advent of the Obama administration. Accordingly,
additional analysis about a nonsensical concept such as a postideological or postpartisan America is not an appropriate investment of
our time or energy. Why waste resources on something that does not
nor cannot exist?

Far more intriguing is the notion of "bipartisanship." It is without
doubt the most misunderstood term in American politics.

The media demands it. The political pundits love it. It polls
extremely well—almost as high as
"change." It is antithetical to its ugly
twin, "partisan." And the voters delivered a firm message they wanted more of
it on November 4, 2008.

*Postpartisan means
the end of partisan
opposition. What could
be more un-American
than a plea to cease
criticism of the ruling
elite?*

So, what *does* it mean?

In Washington, D.C., circa 2009, it
soon became apparent that at least one
aspect of an Obama-style bipartisanship
is less about common ground and more
about mutual respect and enhanced col-
legiality among members of Congress.
As a former congressman and deputy majority whip, I welcome this
attempt at a more civil discourse. Civility should not be confused
with a less partisan environment, however. A more respectful environment does not transform a Capitol Hill culture consumed with
majority/minority status. Regardless of which party gains control,
even innovative ideas, bills, programs, or initiatives will be killed
simply because they emanate from the minority party. The vast majority of voters may wish to believe otherwise, but the partisan culture *always* survives.

To the Winner Goes the Spoils

My more serious objection occurs when the loyal opposition is expected to roll over simply because its party lost an election. Not that
President Obama was wrong in stating that he now gets to do things

his way because he and his party won the 2008 election. To the winner goes the spoils; in this case, an issues agenda Obama, Reid, and Pelosi have advocated since the beginning of their public careers. The platform is apparent for all to see: gigantic government, higher marginal tax rates, centralized authority, environmental extremism, an apologetic and weak foreign policy, and limited economic horizons. It is an agenda that carried the day over two election cycles. It is also an agenda many Americans oppose, regardless of political affiliation. One need look no further than November 2, 2010, for confirmation.

So, what should Republicans have done with the Obama administration's "stimulus" bill? Just gone along because of a popular, charismatic president and his persuasive ways? Signed off after a few slices of pork were eliminated from the pig? Or continued to fight in good faith for what most in the congressional minority believed to be the fundamentals of a true "rescue package": short-term safety net assistance, "shovel-ready" infrastructure projects, tax relief for those who actually pay federal income taxes, and no pork.

A spending binge leading to historic federal budget deficits is the worst possible time to get in touch with one's bipartisan side. Here, getting out of the way to "prove" your bipartisan nature is misplaced emotion. It is also quite dangerous in light of the other serious items on the progressive agenda since January 2007.

Despite the 2008 election, many Americans oppose Obama-inspired policies, if not the personable man himself, as offensive to even centrist sensibilities: a trillion-dollar, pork-filled "stimulus," civil rights for terrorists, ending the use of enhanced interrogation techniques on captured enemy combatants, a newly minted "Fairness Doctrine," the end of secret ballots in union-organizing elections, a protectionist streak on trade, promises of activist judges, dozens of senior policy "czars" answerable to nobody, and trial lawyers gone wild. This is an agenda far out of step with red *and* blue mainstream America. And no charismatic president promoting a media-induced redefinition of "bipartisan" can transform such proposals into "mainstream."

Sometimes, a bipartisan resolution is *not* a sound resolution. Sometimes, walking away from a deal is better than a bad deal. Those of us in the loyal and growing opposition must not be afraid to say it, either.

A related and equally uncomplicated debate revolves around the issue of what "red state America" should root for during the Obama era. Not surprisingly, early in the Obama administration pundits on the left zeroed in on the more aggressive statements issued by leaders of the conservative movement—from Rush Limbaugh and Mark Levin to Sean Hannity and Sarah Palin. In response, reports surfaced about a White House–led effort to impeach the credibility of right-wing talk radio hosts, particularly Limbaugh. Leading this effort was the White House Chief of Staff, Rahm Emanuel, joined by his former Clinton administration buddies Paul Begala and James Carville. Their goal? The marginalization of those who wish to challenge Obama's agenda. No surprise here. These pundits want to perpetuate the image of an embittered, pessimistic right wing dedicated to the failure of everything Obama.

This unique strategy so energized the Obama White House that senior staff did not bother with the usual countercharges of right-wing paranoia. In fact, they happily took ownership of the Limbaugh-inspired messaging strategy. Per Carville, "[I]t's great for us, great for him (Limbaugh), great for the press.... The only people he's not good for are the actual Republicans in Congress."[115] In effect, it was a public marginalization of the messenger, not the message—a well-worn campaign tactic perfected by the Clinton White House. Only time will tell if this hypercynical approach will prove an effective political strategy for an image-sensitive Obama White House. Indeed, the voting public should expect more of this Clintonesque approach in the lead-up to the 2012 presidential election.

Let's Not Take Our Democracy for Granted

Despite this all-too-familiar refrain from the usual suspects and the renewed energy of the left-wing blogosphere, two baseline conclusions should be obvious: first, all Americans should pray for the safety, success, and continued prosperity of the greatest democracy

---

[115] Jonathan Martin, "Rush Job: Inside Dems' Limbaugh plan," *Politico*, March 4, 2009.

in the history of the world—and those prayers and good wishes must extend to the president, his family, and his administration. This should be clear to all, as the most successful democracy in world history continues to be a popular target for modern-day terrorists of all shapes and sizes.

Second, while the "new" New Deal takes shape, and the network cheerleaders for the Obama administration perform their nightly marketing activities, it is incumbent upon all Americans to remember that the stakes remain extraordinarily high—market capitalism, free speech, lower marginal tax burdens, federalism, workplace freedom, success in the war against terror, and American exceptionalism are but a few of our fundamental values at risk during the Obama era.

The 2010 midterm elections and a new Republican House put a stop to the left's Obama-inspired momentum, but it will require a heavy measure of political discipline to win the long-term rhetorical debate against heavy mainstream media opposition. At every turn, those of us within the loyal opposition must oppose the hijacking of an apparently benign, but rhetorically misleading, concept such as bipartisanship. At the same time, we should refuse to indulge the intellectually insufficient notion of a postpartisan political world. As the efforts of the commonsense majority begin to reemerge in middle America, the familiar charge of "insensitivity" to the new political order will be made. As usual, a familiar lesson applies to our response—a direct rejection of the charge and an unwillingness to back down when the hyperaggressive "ism" charges begin anew. I'm not offering a new plan here, but simply reaffirming how, without our commonsense traditional values, our great country loses its greatness, its influence, and goes the way of European-style social democrat countries. The dire need for such an aggressive response is the central thesis of this book.

The rhetoric used by Obama during his initial series of world tours requires further examination. To wit, voters must understand the direct relationship between the administration's full-scale offensive on bipartisanship and the repeated instances where the president has drawn moral equivalency between real, exaggerated, and even imagined American misdeeds and the typically far more egregious actions of other nations.

The common denominator is the passion for approval, regardless of facts or context. On the domestic front, it's the theme of "Let's bypass the endless partisan bickering in order to secure my progressive agenda." As analyzed above, this is a trenchant tactic for an energetic, telegenic leader enjoying a compliant media. The perceived ability to rise above mudslinging and partisan conflict is what makes the approach so effective. In blunt terms, how can the opposition challenge a president who is assumed to occupy the moral high ground? And, if you are going to lose anyway, why not just indulge a popular chief executive? Your reward will be waiting in tomorrow's newspapers, where your new bipartisan buy-in will assuredly receive an approving nod from *The Washington Post* and *The New York Times*.

A vote in support of traditional marriage is deemed hateful toward gays, while harsh criticism directed at a black president is dismissed as racist.

Have any doubt about the foregoing narrative? Witness *Newsweek* editor Evan Thomas' ravings about a newly elected President Obama on MSNBC: "I mean in a way Obama's standing above the country, above, above the world, he's sort of God."[116] So how do *you* think *Newsweek* will treat those who dare oppose "God"?

Yet another aspect of what is not bipartisan is the consistent practice of the left to institute a selective brand of demonization politics—and usurp an emotional verb: hate.

References to "hate speech" now dominate the mainstream media and are used, almost without exception, to characterize right-wing tactics. In this context, over-the-top, hyperaggressive rhetoric directed against President Bush, Sarah Palin, Fox News, or talk radio fails to meet the requisite litmus test. The formula is familiar: take a liberal policy (gay marriage, high marginal tax rates, judicial activism) and declare any criticism of same off-limits. Any violation of this

---

[116] Evan Thomas, *Hardball with Chris Matthews*, MSNBC, June 5, 2009.

policy is automatically deemed "hateful"—and violations can apply to policy or people. Hence, a vote in support of traditional marriage is deemed hateful toward gays, while harsh criticism directed at a black president is dismissed as racist. What an effective but anti-intellectual tool—unilaterally declared rules of engagement used to delegitimize philosophical opposition.

The First to Point Fingers

Further polluting the traditional definition of bipartisanship is the rhetorically deceptive tactic of declaring oneself above the partisan fray while associating the opposition with all things negative. What better example of this dangerous strategy than President Obama's speech in the aftermath of the Tucson, Arizona, shooting spree that left six dead and Congresswoman Gabrielle Giffords (D-AZ) critically injured?

First, the usual suspects spoke immediately after the shootings: Rep. Jim Clyburn (D-SC) cited the Tucson shootings in calling for a renewed Fairness Doctrine (a doctrine that would require equal time for liberal talk radio hosts despite the repeated failures of left-leaning talk shows), while Michael Daly of the *New York Daily News* entitled an essay, "Rep. Gabrielle Giffords' Blood Is on Sarah Palin's Hands after Putting Cross Hair over District."[117]

Gun control leaders in Congress renewed calls for limits on high-capacity ammunition magazines, and Rep. Robert A. Brady (D-PA) proposed a bill that would make it a federal crime to use language or symbols that could be interpreted or "perceived" as inciting violence against a federal official.

These usual suspects carry the moniker because they are so predictable. They never disappoint in their ability to take advantage of a tragic event. They simply draw a straight line between the event and a conservative (person or group) target, without regard to supporting facts. Objective evidence to the contrary is dismissed or conveniently overlooked.

---

[117] Michael Daly, "Rep. Gabrielle Giffords' Blood Is on Sarah Palin's Hands after Putting Cross Hair over District," *New York Daily News*, January 9, 2011.

This, then, was an ideal opportunity for the hoped-for postideological president to take a stand against political opportunism; a chance to distinguish himself from the hyperaggressive elements of his own party engaged in a rush to judgment against any and all things Second Amendment, tea party, or Sarah Palin.

He failed, sort of...

First, in clear terms, he correctly described what was *not* the cause of a troubled killer's outrage:

> Scripture tells us that there is evil in the world, and that terrible things happen for reasons that defy human understanding. In the words of Job, "when I looked for light, then came darkness." Bad things happen, and we have to guard against simple explanations in the aftermath. For the truth is that none of us can know exactly what triggered this vicious attack. None of us can know with any certainty what might have stopped these shots from being fired, or what thoughts lurked in the inner recesses of a violent man's mind.[118]

Elegant words that could have served to diminish the vitriol from the left. However, he also imparted a series of observations targeted to aggressive political rhetoric:

> But at a time when our discourse has become so sharply polarized—at a time when we are far too eager to lay the blame for all that ails the world at the feet of those who happen to think differently than we do—it's important for us to pause for a moment and make sure that we're talking with each other in a way that heals, not a way that wounds.[119]

And then, the "perfect" (for him, at least) rhetorical paragraph where the president both disassociates himself from the political finger-pointing and again issues a clarion call for a more low temperature discourse on politics and policy:

---

[118] Office of the President of the United States, "Remarks by the President at a Memorial Service for the Victims of the Shooting in Tucson, Arizona," news release, January 12, 2011.
[119] Ibid.

But what we can't do is use this tragedy as one more occasion to turn on each other. That we cannot do. That we cannot do. As we discuss these issues, let each of us do so with a good dose of humility. Rather than pointing fingers or assigning blame, let's use this occasion to expand our moral imaginations, to listen to each other more carefully, to sharpen our instincts for empathy and remind ourselves of all the ways that our hopes and dreams are bound together.[120]

Such spoken words only seek to divert focus to a narrative that meets the policy and rhetorical goals of the speaker. In other words, President Obama was attempting to imply indirectly that this was a partisan issue and the right had something to do with it. To paraphrase Rahm Emanuel, never waste an opportunity to take advantage of a crisis to reestablish the political high ground.

Commentary about how we talk to one another has no relevance to the Tucson shootings. The shooter, Jared Lee Loughner, had no connection to any far-right group. Published reports painted the picture of a wildly disturbed individual who was decidedly left-wing during his high school and college years—only three years removed from the attack.

Taking the Moral High Ground?

President Obama's use of speeches to spin left-wing rhetoric has happened before. His persistent mantra of moral equivalency in the context of American foreign policy, for example, derives from the same desire to rise above ugly conflict in order to render judgment from a higher plane. A permanent place on the moral high ground is always advantageous in high-stakes political conflicts. Pretending that transparently different government actions and policies should be assessed on morally equal terms is Obama's chosen means to *always* own this high ground.[121]

---

[120] Ibid.

[121] Recall the horrific reviews in the aftermath of the memorial service for Senator Paul Wellstone (D-MN), during which a respectful send-off degenerated into a partisan rally in support of progressives and their agenda.

Of course, once moral equivalency is established, appropriate apologies must follow. And since American transgressions are now magnified on the world stage, those apologies must be all-encompassing—the better to assure our enemies that America better understands its demons because we now have come to grips with so many of our own. Accordingly, apologies regularly pour from Obama for everything: Gitmo, detainee interrogation, slavery, violation of basic American values, and the always reliable U.S. arrogance—a popular theme during the Obama administration's early entreaties to the anti-U.S. world.

Students of political rhetoric see the answer as self-evident: moral equivalency is the first cousin to bipartisanship. Both are meant to make one feel better through the dumbing-down of historical perspective and events.

This tendency to engage a remorseful, apologetic tone and draw at times ludicrous equivalency between dramatically different historical events and circumstances has become familiar fodder for the right. Indeed, the right-wing blogosphere went into overdrive during Obama's initial pilgrimages to Europe and the Middle East.

In Germany, same-day visits to the infamous Buchenwald death camp and the city of Dresden seemed to imply equivalency between an infamous Nazi concentration camp and a civilian bombing attack.

In Cairo, Obama drew clear comparisons between the Holocaust and the plight of the Palestinians on the West Bank and Gaza. Also in Cairo, treatment of Palestinians by the Israelis was compared to the status of African Americans in America prior to the advent of civil rights.

In an even more absurd context, the dismal state of women's rights in major parts of the Muslim world was likened to the status of American women in the twenty-first century.

Almost immediately, conservative commentators from Charles Krauthammer and Michael Barone to Jonathan Tobin and Fred Barnes responded with eloquent analyses about the destructive consequences to the United States of this apologetic tone and limitless desire for political and cultural correctness. Many of these same pundits wondered *why* the denigration of America and American institutions must accompany diplomatic entreaties to the world community. Students of political rhetoric see the answer as self-evident: moral equivalency is the *first cousin* to bipartisanship. Both are meant to make one feel better through the dumbing-down of historical perspective and events. For the "Blame America First" crowd, there can be no better equation. It's the juice that keeps on giving, through an endless series of apologies and self-flagellation. As an added bonus, the notion of everything being generally equal further denigrates the notion of American exceptionalism Think about it: How can America and its institutions be exceptional if our policy sins are no different than those of notorious regimes and terrorist organizations?

True bipartisanship is a consensus on policy goals, not strategies or priorities or means. While it abhors the politics of personal destruction, it recognizes that bipartisan acquaintance is *not* the normal state of things in a vibrant democracy. Dissent is a fundamental right of a free people. Loyal opposition is typically not motivated by hate but a desire to attain or recapture power. And moral equivalency is a dangerous game to play in a world where evil regimes are on perpetual watch for signs of American weakness.

A boundless desire to placate foreign rivals has never been a successful guiding principle of American foreign policy. Drawing inaccurate historical analogies in order to patronize unfriendly regimes can only lead to trouble in the long run. I hope that these historical lessons will not be forgotten before an Obama-led, media-driven re-education campaign can gain long-term traction within our political lexicon.

Taking On the
Living Wage Movement

THE SO-CALLED LIVING WAGE MOVEMENT arrived in Maryland for keeps in 2004. It appeared in the form of Senate Bill 621—"State Procurement Contracts—Living Wage" The bill required any business with a state contract for services in excess of $100,000 to pay its employees a state-mandated living wage. The legislation further set Maryland's living wage for 2005 at $10.50 per hour, with annual adjustments to be completed by the Commissioner of Labor and Industry. As usual when it came to disastrous initiatives from the far left, the political stakes at play were quite high—passage of the bill would make Maryland the *first state in the country* to adopt the living wage as a statewide policy. In other words, famously progressive Maryland would again lead the way in a relentless campaign to expand the reach of government. This time, though, through wage rates typically set by the private sector.

211

Progressives jumped on the living wage bandwagon in an aggressive way. As expected, a "dream team" coalition of liberal advocacy group Progressive Maryland, ACORN, organized labor, and several leading Democratic legislators became prime cheerleaders for the living wage movement.

Predictably, the opposition was led by business lobbyists who well understood how a living wage law would place small businesses at a competitive disadvantage in bidding for state contracts. A position paper issued by the Maryland Chamber of Commerce pointed out that the state of Maryland failed to pay its own entry-level employees at the $11.30 per hour rate mandated by the legislation. Private sector advocates asked why the General Assembly would consider inflating the cost of state contracts when the state was facing a multibillion-dollar structural deficit. For me, the question was more profound—the state's already-damaged business reputation would be further soiled by such a radical measure. We had been the first state to pass the so-called "Walmart bill"—a health care mandate under which only one employer in Maryland—anti-union Walmart—would be required to pay a percentage of its gross income to the state as reimbursement for increased Medicaid costs. Maryland had the fourth-highest personal income tax burden in the nation. Our reputation for regulatory interference was already well established. The General Assembly had previously overridden my veto of a proposed increase in Maryland's minimum wage. How much additional damage could be inflicted on Maryland's business image and low-wage workforce before it reached the point of no return?[122]

Fortunately, at least in the short term,[123] rational economic thought carried the day. My veto was sustained. Even Senate President Mike Miller conceded that making Maryland the first "living wage" state "sends a wrong message to the business community."[124]

---

[122] Maybe June 2011 marked the metaphoric point of no return as Maryland fell to fiftieth—dead last—in job creation, according to a U.S. Labor Department report.

[123] In Maryland, all good things do end—and rather quickly. On May 8, 2007, newly elected Democratic Governor Martin O'Malley made Maryland the first "living wage" state.

[124] David Nitkin, "2 Bills' Vetoes Likely to Hold," *The Baltimore Sun*, January 11, 2005.

Nationwide Movement

Our short-term success in Maryland, however, did not disrupt the nationwide momentum in support of living wage initiatives. Similar bills gained political momentum with the national Democratic sweeps of the 2006 and 2008 election cycles. To date, there are more than 140 living wage laws throughout the country.

The "why" behind the popularity of these laws is obvious—who in their right mind would deny a minimum level of subsistence to the most marginal among us? Who could be so heartless as to deny anyone's right to earn a decent hourly wage in the wealthiest country in the world?

Well, almost without exception, it is those mean-spirited Republicans who are more than happy to stand in opposition. Yes, once again the right is automatically placed on the political defensive. Who indeed but cruel, conservative Republicans could deny such a "fundamental" right to the less fortunate among us?

The political rhetoric is identical to the minimum wage debate. And class warfare is the cornerstone of the public debate: in the one corner, warmhearted liberals and their organized labor friends are using all the familiar talking points on behalf of the "repressed" worker. In the other, bottom-line businessmen and their legislative enablers going about the business of undercutting wages at every opportunity in order to make that last buck.

Do the Math

Unlike the dramatic stage of politics, in the real world simple economics can help balance the rhetorical mismatch between left and right. A graduate degree in economics is not required to understand how government-mandated, artificially high wage rates negatively impact marginal workers—and those small and often minority-owned businesses that employ those with limited skills. Accordingly, most reputable studies reflect what a basic understanding of competitive markets would lead one to conclude: that artificially set living wage mandates harm poor workers living at or near the poverty line because of job elimination or the shifting of marginal jobs to more skilled laborers.

So, the challenge is indeed familiar: how to use economics effectively in the never-ending battle against those who claim to own the moral high ground? Put another way, what is a Republican or conservative Democrat to do when confronted with the emotionalism of the "hearts and minds" campaign on behalf of the oppressed worker?

My response, and the only option I could think of, was to stress living wage laws' negative impact on entry-level jobs. The economic analysis is easy to paint. Just about everybody can understand how a higher wage law impacts marginal laborers—those at the lower end of the income scale. These marginal laborers are disproportionately young, minority, and unskilled. They are negatively impacted by any change that makes it more expensive for employers to hire. They are always the first to be fired during down times since their marginal worth to the business is minimal. In effect, a wage rate set above marketplace value guarantees no job at all; why would any business make a decision to hire if it knew that such an act would result in a loss to the bottom line? A further unpleasant consequence: the least skilled and most problematic laborers are the most visible victims. How ironic that these same victims are the most vulnerable political targets for the proponents of these ill-conceived laws.

Even more ironic is the behavior of most African American legislators. Almost without exception, black caucuses around the country are enthusiastic in their support for living wages, even though study after study details the negative impact living wage laws have on marginal and disproportionately minority workers. These workers' self-avowed representatives in Congress and state legislatures ignore this reality and instead provide a steady stream of votes for the implementation of a living wage.

My experience with the Maryland General Assembly was no exception, as only one member of the Maryland Legislative Black Caucus voted to sustain my veto of Senate Bill 621. This clear-cut divide is but another stunning example of how class warfare doctrine often trumps basic economics—and real-world experience. Unfortunately, the almost unanimous support for living wage laws from liberal caucuses and interest groups ensures that the intended beneficiaries will always suffer. And only confrontational, direct campaigning from small business interests will educate voters about the dire consequences. The ability to sustain a veto does not hurt, either.

There is a further worrisome note on the living wage movement. As with any hyperaggressive lobby, it is consistently changing its modus operandi and goals. What was initially limited to businesses with government contracts has expanded to private entities having no connection to municipalities or states. Moreover, the next generation of wage legislation has begun—a "benefit surcharge" added to the already-inflated base wage rate. This follows the natural progression of such feel-good legislation and is another example of how bad ideas always grow absent a determined willingness to confront and defeat them.

Over the past decade, as 'living wage" became a rally cry within the ranks of labor and other hard-left interest groups, a more determined response has emerged from business advocates. To its great credit, the U.S. Chamber of Commerce has led the charge. Local chambers and other small business lobbies have joined the chorus in organizing opposition to these job-killing ordinances—never an easy task.

The election of Barack Obama was a major wake-up call for small business entrepreneurs in our country. ACORN's former attorney is now president of the United States, assisted immeasurably by the increasingly radical Service Employees International Union and other like-minded public unions. Their demand for seductive yet job-killing measures, such as living wage legislation, will remain front and center. The 2010 midterm election and the willingness of new Republican governors to confront these initiatives have most certainly slowed the momentum. So has a slow-developing recovery buffeted by sustained high unemployment. Nevertheless, these zealots do not stand down. They have been energized by the incredible growth of public sector unions over the past decade. They played a significant part in electing a president of their ideological bent. They know what sounds good to the average person, particularly during an economic downturn. They understand and practice the art of grassroots organizing. They practice an aggressive form of in-your-face class warfare sure to scare the average moderate legislator.

They live to expand government's reach into every nook and cranny of our economy. And only a sustained, long-term communications strategy aimed at the hearts, minds, and paychecks of working-class America will defeat them.

Concluding Thoughts

SO, CAN A REENERGIZED commonsense majority get its collective act together in order to restore a strong and vibrant America?

It *can* be done, but a newly minted, perverse interpretation of "voting rights" presents a very real roadblock to our road map.

It was an inherited medical condition from my dad that brought it all home to me. You see, seasonal ragweed allergies in the spring and fall have been the bane of my life since early childhood. Any fellow sufferer knows all too well the runny nose, red eyes, and constant sneezing that make millions miserable. Fortunately, over-the-counter remedies have improved over the years, and, in my case, Claritin-D has proven to be the most effective medication out of all the alternatives.

Each time I purchase Claritin-D, I am required to produce my Maryland driver's license—governor or not! The stated reason for this quite minimal imposition on my privacy is the apparent ease with which certain ingredients in Claritin-D can be used in the manufacture of methamphetamine, or "crystal meth."

The small inconvenience to me and a rational explanation by the pharmacist makes this a nonevent. But consider this: filling in a logbook, showing a photo ID, and providing a signature are federally imposed safeguards for purchasing a popular allergy medicine, yet in Maryland (and many other states) the requirements accompanying the single most important right of an American citizen—the act of voting—are . . . next to nothing.

The lack of precautionary measures at the ballot box gives rise to easily accomplished voter fraud. This is a view I strongly espoused as governor and it was met with a hail of criticism. The most vivid example of this was a 2006 interview with the editorial board of a large, locally owned African American newspaper in Baltimore. Of particular interest to me was a racial insensitivity critique lobbed at me, charging that mandatory photo identification at the polls acts as a disincentive to vote and is discriminatory against racial minorities. I reject that notion. It is not discriminatory against racial minorities or the disadvantaged poor, or senior citizens, for that matter.

The central thrust of this indictment is that these groups are disenfranchised because they lack the necessary means, such as reliable photo identification, to vote. Really? Most citizens possess some sort of photo identification in order to live legally in the United States. Indeed, it is increasingly difficult to do *anything* without some form of photo identification. My Claritin-D example may be the most obvious, but everything from boarding an airplane to securing government benefits requires that one produce reliable identification.

And there is no shortage of documents that would pass muster under state identification laws, for example—driver's license, passport, naturalization papers, and state, federal, tribal, and student identification cards. Further, many states allow limited but clearly appropriate exceptions for those unable or unwilling to comply: stalking victims, nursing- or retirement-home residents, or those who claim exception on religious grounds.

Even with all these easily obtained documents for legal residents, many states require only minimum requirements: a photo ID for first-time voters only or nonphoto documents such as fishing licenses, adoption papers, gun permits, bank statements, or utility bills.

It has become a political issue used to champion the poor, crying foul on behalf of economically challenged constituencies. In fact, today's left has transformed such charges into an art form. Witness, for example, the left-wing *Toledo Blade*, whose editorial board labeled Ohio's voter ID law a "ruse" whose "true intent seems to be to make it harder for some Ohioans to vote" and should be identified as "the 21st-century equivalent of a poll tax."[125] Second prize for over-the-top rhetoric goes to Wisconsin Democratic Senator Jon Erpenbach, who charged Republicans with an "indefensible" attempt to "wreck the Democratic Party."[126] The issue? A Wisconsin bill to require a photo ID in order to vote on Election Day.

Voter identification fraud is difficult to prosecute precisely because the primary tool required to prove the allegation (authentic identification) is denied to election officials by a majority of the states.

Similar race-based rhetoric followed the 2006 House passage of a federal photo ID bill, with the likes of Nancy Pelosi and Harry Reid playing the Jim Crow–era poll tax analogy to the hilt.

A Circular Argument

Political correctness may have succeeded in diminishing a wide range of conventional cultural values, but it hasn't diverted a clear majority of Americans from continuing to support the notion that some legitimate form of photo identification should be required in order to vote. It is a solid position. After all, everyone gets protected in the process, including the elderly, minority, and poor voters—the alleged victims of photo ID laws.

The other charge by the left is that Election Day fraud is rare, and cases of voter impersonation are even more rare, so why bother with so-called restrictive ID measures?

---

[125] Editorial, "21st-Century Poll Tax," *The Toledo Blade*, July 13, 2011.
[126] "State Senate Passes voter ID Bill, sends to Walker," The Associated Press, May 19, 2011.

But the circular nature of this argument is transparent: voter identification fraud is difficult to prove precisely because the primary tool required to prove the allegation (authentic identification) is denied to election officials by a majority of the states. The Seventh Circuit Court of Appeals noted as much in upholding an Indiana photo identification law (subsequently affirmed by the Supreme Court in 2008):

> The absence of prosecutions is explained by the endemic under-enforcement of minor criminal laws (minor as they appear to the public and prosecutors, at all events) and by the extreme difficulty of apprehending a voter impersonator. He enters the polling place, gives a name that is not his own, votes, and leaves. If later it is discovered that the name he gave is that of a dead person, no one at the polling place will remember the face of the person who gave that name, and if someone did remember it, what would he do with the information?[127]

Many of the conservative and/or libertarian think tanks (particularly The Heritage Foundation) have arrived at similar conclusions after serious empirical analysis. Yet progressives of all stripes continue to sound the trumpet of race- and class-based intimidation despite a lack of evidence supporting the supposition that voter identification requirements diminish voter turnout.

The screams of bloody murder from the left may have one credible aside—photo identification requirements have a chilling effect on the ability of illegal aliens to cast ballots. This result may not be what the advocates of illegal immigration intended, but it sure makes the rest of us feel better. Of course, this is not the case in states that have allowed illegal aliens to obtain driver's licenses. How do I know? Well, I live in one of those states.

In the vast majority of states that take ballot security seriously, the goal of every election administrator is to eliminate all non-qualified individuals from voting, a goal made more difficult by the

---

[127] *William Crawford, et al, v. Marion County Election Board, et al*, Nos. 06-2218, 06-2317 (7th Cir. 2007).

increasing popularity of early voting and same-day registration laws. Nevertheless, "one person–one legal vote" must be the proverbial line in the sand if we intend to remain serious about our rights.

America has fought many wars since 1776. Approximately 1.2 million men and women have died in the course of our country's military conflicts over that time. Millions more have been wounded or scarred by the brutality of warfare. These soldiers were asked to make the ultimate sacrifice on behalf of a nation defined by freedom and democracy. This democracy is, in turn, constructed on a guarantee of free and accurate elections. They deserve our very best efforts at protecting this guarantee. feel-good rhetoric notwithstanding.

A principle that should be easy to articulate and defend is no longer. Concerted efforts to weaken our voter identification laws have become commonplace around the country. As is the case with so many of the issues raised in this book, I'm raising a call to action here. It is time for the commonsense majority to take back the fundamental issue of allowing only U.S. citizens to vote. The senselessness of the argument promoted by protectors of illegal voting needs to be exposed: modest identification requirements have nothing to do with race or class bias.

The Bigger Picture

My experience with the issue of photo identification is but a subcontext for a much broader project: the foregoing blueprint in support of a commonsense conservative majority in the run-up to a historic presidential election. It is a campaign that will play out against the backdrop of a dramatic economic slowdown and a unique, nontraditional war, with an American public seemingly undecided over what type of commitment it will take to regain our cultural and economic dominance.

There is a well-analyzed subculture on the left whose reflexive reaction to American cultural norms (let alone U.S. foreign policy engagements) is to stress the negative implications of U.S. policy and culture, to always view action taken in defense of America and U.S. interests as somehow violating an unwritten world charter. Many years ago, Jeane Kirkpatrick, our ambassador to the United Nations under President

Reagan, famously labeled this group of usual suspects the "blame America first-ers," since their first response to American action around the world was to not only oppose it but to assume that America was at fault for whatever grievances were at issue at the moment. A similar presumption applied to domestic events and institutions during the Bush administration, with attacks on American culture and values typically carried out in highly emotional terms.

On issues of foreign policy, President Bush labeled this camp the "permission slip" crowd, as though America must first ask permission of other countries in order to defend ourselves and protect our interests. One wonders how this group would have reacted to Pearl Harbor. What foreign policy positions would they have advocated on December 8, 1941?

One persistent attribute is a masterful, if not transparent, use of association to demonize and denigrate. For example, one need not search long to locate consistent references to Hitler or Nazism in the new left's critique of those on the right who dare to challenge liberal orthodoxy, from global warming to domestic surveillance to Islamic radicalism to multiculturalism. A few of my favorites of recent vintage:

- Minnesota Congressman Keith Ellison, a newly elected Democrat and America's first Muslim member of Congress, told a group of atheists in 2007 that President Bush responded to the 9/11 attacks in much the same way that Adolf Hitler responded to fires that destroyed the German Reichstag: "It's almost like the Reichstag fire....After the Reichstag was burned, they blamed the Communists for it and it put the leader [Hitler] of that country in a position where he could basically have authority to do whatever he wanted."[128]
- Former Vice President Al Gore, in a heated spepech in June 2004, compared the Bush administration's communications operation to Nazi "Brown Shirts": "The administration works closely with a network of rapid-response digital Brown Shirts who work to

---

[128] Katherine Kersten, "Keith Ellison Goes Overboard," RealClearPolitics.com, July 12, 2007, www.realclearpolitics.com/articles/2007/07/keith_ellison_goes_overboard.html (accessed September 1, 2011).

pressure reporters and their editors for undermining support for our troops."[129]

- Then Senator Robert Byrd (D-WV), in opposing a Republican Senate rule change contemplated by GOP leaders that would deny Democrats the ability to filibuster judicial nominations, compared the move to a 1933 law that provided Adolf Hitler limitless power: "We, unlike Nazi Germany or Mussolini's Italy, have never stopped being a nation of laws, not of men. But witness how men with motives and a majority can manipulate law to cruel and unjust ends. Historian Alan Bullock writes that Hitler's dictatorship rested on the constitutional foundation of a single law, the Enabling Law. Hitler needed a two-thirds vote to pass that law, and he cajoled his opposition in the Reichstag to support it. Bullock writes that 'Hitler was prepared to promise anything to get his bill through, with the appearances of legality preserved intact.' And he succeeded."[130]

- More recently, Congressman Steve Cohen sought to draw a parallel between Hitler's minister of propaganda, Joseph Goebbels, and GOP opposition to Obamacare: "They don't like the truth so they summarily dismiss it. They say it's a government takeover of health care, a big lie. Just like Goebbels. You say it enough, you repeat the lie, you repeat the lie, you repeat the lie, and eventually people believe it."[131]

Of course, even Hitler analogies can grow tiresome. At these times, that old reliable analogy—race—gets reinfused into the equation. It seems as though there is no end to the opportunities presented by this popular tactic. Case in point: the infamous 2000 NAACP National Voter Fund commercial that attempted to connect then Governor George W. Bush with the racially motivated homicide of

---

[129] Greg Pollowitz, "Al Gore Bans the Media," *The National Review*, September 20, 2007.

[130] "Media Covered Controversial Comments by Democrats More Extensively than Republicans," Media Matters for America, March 10, 2005, http://mediamatters.org/research/200503110001 (accessed September 2, 2011).

[131] Kyle Drennen, "MSNBC: Rep. Cohen Compares Mike Pence to Goebbels, No Challenge from Ed Schultz," Media Research Center, January 21, 2011, http://newsbusters.org/blogs/kyle-drennen/2011/01/21/msnbc-rep-cohen-compares-mike-pence-goebbels-no-challenge-ed-schultz (accessed September 2, 2011).

James Byrd Jr., who was horrifically dragged to death in Jasper, Texas, in 1998. The ad in question featured a chain being raked along a dirt road with a voice-over by Byrd's daughter, Renee Mullins, stating, "On June 7, 1998, in Texas, my father was killed. He was beaten, chained, and then dragged three miles to his death, all because he was black. So when Governor George W. Bush refused to support hate-crime legislation, it was like my father was killed all over again. Call Governor George W. Bush and tell him to support hate-crime legislation. We won't be dragged away from our future." The genesis of this spectacular smear job was Bush's opposition to a proposed new hate crimes statute (Texas already had a law that increased the penalty for crimes committed out of prejudice toward any race or group) that sought to increase penalties only for crimes committed out of prejudice against minorities and homosexuals.

The constant comparison between conservatives and the most evil dictator the world has ever known, or the tying together of a legitimate policy position (opposing newly invented "hate thought" statutes) with murder, is no accident. It is a powerful tool. It speaks to the alleged lack of a moral compass possessed by those who would dare question the convictions advocated by the left, all of which pertain to the fundamental intolerance of the new left in contemporary American politics. How else to phrase it? The spirit of intolerance previously associated with extremists of the far right is today more accurately associated with the contemporary left! And the transition occurred over a relatively short period of time. All one need observe is a protest against the Reserve Officers' Training Corps on a college campus, the persistent charge of ethnocentricism lodged against those who wish to enforce our immigration laws, the disrespectful behavior directed at former Secretary of State Condoleezza Rice during a college commencement, the Boy Scouts of America being forced to defend itself for meetings held in public elementary schools, or, closer to my home, potential lieutenant governor Michael Steele being dismissed as bringing nothing more to the ticket than the color of his skin.

Stand Up for America

As I have written repeatedly in this book, the incessant intolerance of our day can only be met and defeated by an equally principled public stand: actually, a hyperaggressive counterattack against the attempted hijacking of our cultural, social, and political values. Here, the act of "taking on" the burden means just that—a willingness to bear unjustified criticism, including the strength of character to watch one's reputation torched by the forces of political correctness. There is an upside, however: once resisted by the equal or greater force of a commonsense majority, the ferocity of the attacks tends to diminish. The temperature decreases because the emotional charges—"insensitivity," "racism," "Hitler-like"—lack the facts and substantive evidence required for acceptance by a majority of Americans—at least so far. The bottom line is that the ability to minimize the "staying power" of the most emotional indictments (racism, class warfare, intolerance) will decide the ultimate winner of our raging culture war.

The commonsense part of the equation is not the sole property of the right, either. Regardless of political identification, I believe most Americans tend to support the core viewpoints expressed in this book, when properly articulated and defended in the public arena:

- Politically correct language is often quite silly—few people expect an "offense-less society"; the all-too-easily-offended divert our attention away from serious instances of sexism, racism, and discrimination. Accordingly, it is increasingly clear that advocates of political correctness perform a disservice to those they allegedly wish to help.
- For far too long in our history, a racially segregated America indulged racist tactics to the detriment of its black citizens; today, the race card is used to create another type of uneven playing field, this one using race and class warfare to denigrate conservative and free market–oriented black candidates and intellectuals. It seeks to impose an ideological litmus test prior to conferring race identification. The unfortunate few who fail the test are banished to "race purgatory" and stuck with the label of "not really black." With rare exceptions, the elected

and self-proclaimed leaders of "Black America" permit this type of racial profiling to fester, without adverse consequences. As such, the race card is today used quite often to create an uneven playing field, thereby furthering racial anxiety and conflict; it is too easily manipulated in order to denigrate black conservative politicians and intellectuals. The logical conclusion: we remain light-years away from Dr. King's historic admonition to judge others according to the content of their character rather than the color of their skin.

- Too many white and black politicians pay lip service to the plight of young, poor, mostly black inner-city students sentenced to the worst public schools. Many of these offenders act to placate public education unions so frequently opposed to the very reforms that lead to better education outcomes for kids in marginal circumstances. In most cases, the act of paying lip service on the students' behalf guarantees a "consequence-less" political outcome in which the same politicians get reelected and generation after generation of our urban poor fail to receive an adequate education. Without a new civil rights revolution demanding fundamental reforms and consequential accountability in our worst-performing public school systems, our society will continue to sentence most members of the so-called "underclass" to perpetual poverty.

- Even in the cable news–induced world of 24/7 news coverage, most readers of newspapers expect to read fact-based stories in the news section and opinion-backed pieces of opposing positions on the editorial and op-ed pages; they also have a right to expect ideologically motivated writers to refrain from making up quotes or story lines in support of their views. These must be minimum requirements for all who seek to avail themselves of the constitutionally protected right to freedom of the press.

- Most parents of teenage daughters are frustrated by glitzy ads so often directed at young girls by today's Hollywood image makers and record producers; most understand sleazy messages directed at impressionable young minds contribute to the epidemic of teenage addiction and underage births. Sex sells, and always will, but why must the targeted buyer be a thirteen-year-old girl?

- Most adults view marriage as a foundational institution central to our Judeo-Christian heritage, and limited to one man and one woman. This widely held view in no way conflicts with the very legitimate debate surrounding the issue of what bundles of rights should be provided to nontraditional couples, either homosexual or heterosexual.

- Most small businesspeople expect business and industry organizations to act in their members' best interests, even when the odds are long and the election of the most supportive candidate is difficult; the last thing small business entrepreneurs should expect is for industry groups to support those who oppose a growth and opportunity agenda simply to curry favor with the probable winners. Far-left unions such as teachers associations would never consider such a tactic; why are their philosophical opponents unable to do the same?

- Free, transparent markets do a far better job than government when it comes to setting the price of goods, services, and wages. Wage and price controls do not and have not worked anywhere they have been tried. Similarly, governmental attempts at mandating artificially high wages do not generate a higher standard of living among marginal workers. Most Americans understand this economic fact of life: only individuals create wealth through their toil and talents. Any pretense otherwise is simply emotionalism dressed up as public policy.

- The tea party–generated determination to finally reform out-of-control entitlement spending is indeed refreshing but not entirely new to Washington—there have been elements of both parties willing to engage in the past. What makes the present situation so historic is the number of members of Congress, mostly House freshmen, dedicated to doing what everyone knows needs to be done, future attack ads and fierce establishment criticism notwithstanding. Further, this grassroots movement has changed debt limit politics, perhaps forever. Prior to 2011, debt limit increases were never linked to budget cuts in such a transparent way. In light of the strategy's success, this connection may very well become the new modus operandi for Congress and the executive branch. In effect, there is now a brand-new avenue for bipartisan budget hawks forever on the hunt for new ways to control federal spending. It's about time; public debt at all levels is truly unsustainable, a fact of life now recognized by a majority of commonsense Americans.

- Most observers now view the great homeownership crusades of the 1990s as a monumental failure; the promise of a mortgage for everyone regardless of one's ability to make monthly payments has led to a historic devaluation of our housing market and a credit squeeze of epic proportions. From 2008 to 2010, more than a million Americans lost their homes due to foreclosure. Feel-good themes from Washington, D.C., and some bad actors in the industry combined to bring us an economic contagion that keeps on giving. Going forward, we must have the internal fortitude to recognize that the availability of credit in a market economy must have *some* relation to the consumers' ability to pay. This basic law of economics cannot be suspended even where the policy goal (in this case, homeownership) is so politically attractive. As the man said, if it sounds too good to be true, it usually is—especially in Washington, D.C.

- Most Americans understand the "war" on drugs never had a chance to succeed since we are the enemy; we set the price and market for illegal substances due to our limitless demand for prohibited substances. Parents of all stripes have a less draconian view of criminal sanctions to be imposed because that substance abuser is just as likely to be the wealthy suburban kid as the poor urban kid. It follows that rehabilitation-based programs will be understood, supported, and received far better today than twenty years ago.

- We are more than 230 years into the most dynamic democracy the world has ever witnessed and yet we still fail to guarantee that only eligible citizens vote on Election Day. This despite cutting-edge technology that allows for instantaneous commercial transactions and communications around the world. It's embarrassing, and the defenders of the status quo must be called to account.

I am an optimist by nature. Dangerous societal trends can turn around. Common sense is an accepted part of our lexicon because a majority of individuals possess the same or similar opinions. In many cases "common" is related to "reflexive," as in a reflexive desire to protect the institution of marriage, a reflexive desire to judge others based on merit rather than color, or the reflexive opposition to outside forces that threaten all we hold near and dear in American culture.

It has been fun to replay instances in which I sought to contest political coalitions and their pet agendas so often aligned against majority positions but increasingly aggressive in their approach. The fact that most of these political battles played out on a public stage in a dark blue state added a touch of spice—and a few sleepless nights. The fights were usually well worth the effort; it is always worthwhile to fight for a cause you believe in. Hopefully, in the near future, a revolution of commonsense-inspired reason *will* occur—and the ideals expressed in this book will live to fight another day. It really is time to turn *this* car around.

Thousands await the swearing in of Maryland's sixtieth governor, January 15, 2003.

About the Author

ROBERT L. EHRLICH, JR. is a partner with the Atlanta firm of King & Spalding. His opinion pieces have appeared in many of America's leading newspapers and journals, including *The Washington Post, The Baltimore Sun, The Washington Times, Washington Examiner,* and *National Review*.

He is a former governor of Maryland, United States congressman, and state legislator. He lives with his wife, Kendel, and sons, Drew and Joshua, in Annapolis, Maryland.

Index